Animals as Guides for the Soul

DISCARD

ANIMALS
AS
GUIDES
FOR THE
SOUL

▲

Stories of Life-Changing Encounters

▼

SUSAN CHERNAK McELROY

BALLANTINE   WELLSPRING

The Ballantine Publishing Group · New York

A Ballantine Wellspring Book
Published by The Ballantine Publishing Group

Copyright © 1998 by Susan Chernak McElroy

www.randomhouse.com/BB/

Grateful acknowledgment is made to the following for permission to reprint previously published material:

Delacorte Press and Elaine Markson Literary Agency, Inc: Excerpt from WHEN ELEPHANTS WEEP by Jeffrey Masson and Susan McCarthy. Copyright © 1995 by Jeffrey Moussaieff Masson and Susan McCarthy. British Commonwealth rights administered by Elaine Markson Literary Agency, Inc. Reprinted by permission of Delacorte Press, a division of Bantam Doubleday Dell Publishing Group, Inc. and Elaine Markson Literary Agency, Inc.

Earthstewards Network: Excerpts from *Warriors of the Heart* by Danaan Parry. Reprinted by permission of Earthstewards Network.

Alfred A Knopf, Inc. and National Committee of Gibran: Excerpts from "On Friendship" and "On Pain" from *The Prophet* by Kahlil Gibran. Copyright © 1923 by Kahlil Gibran and renewed 1951 by Administrators C.T.A. of Kahlil Gibran Estate and Mary G. Gibran. Reprinted by permission of Alfred A. Knopf, Inc.

Chocolate Chelsea: A Canine of Courage by Patty Aguirre printed courtesy of Delta Society® from "Natural Connections," a contest sponsored by Naturistics®.

LIBRARY OF CONGRESS CATALOGING-IN-PUBLICATION DATA
McElroy, Susan Chernak, 1952—
    Animals as guides for the soul : stories of life-changing encounters /
Susan Chernak McElroy.—1st ed.
        p.   cm.
    "A Ballantine Wellspring book."
    Includes bibliographical references.
    ISBN 0-345-42403-4 (alk. paper)
    1. Human-animal relationships.   2. Animals—Psychological
aspects.   3. Pets—Psychological aspects.   4. Pet owners—Psychology.
I. Title.
QL85.M33   1998
636.088'7—dc21   98-29805

Manufactured in the United States of America
Text design by Mary A. Wirth
First Edition: November 1998

10 9 8 7 6 5 4 3 2 1

For my mother, Hermine Chernak,
who taught me to always feed the animals first

CONTENTS

ACKNOWLEDGMENTS   ix

INTRODUCTION
Teaching What We Most Want to Know   3

CHAPTER ONE
Brightstar Farm: Between Two Rivers   15

CHAPTER TWO
A Blessing from the Animals   27

CHAPTER THREE
A Language of the Heart: Communicating with Animals   64

CHAPTER FOUR
Service   94

CHAPTER FIVE
Messengers, Dreams, and Visions   140

CHAPTER SIX
Grief, Guilt, and Atonement   183

CHAPTER SEVEN
Transforming the Relationship Between Humans and Animals   225

EPILOGUE
The Spirit of Brightstar   284

RESOURCES   288

Once again, I have the honor of stewarding a book into the world. If not for countless friends, colleagues, and miracle workers whose skills and inspiration continue to support me in this work, there could not possibly *be* this second book. It is my great joy to acknowledge their contributions here.

From the very beginning of my "book work," I have been blessed with great editors—Maureen R. Michelson and Joanne Wyckoff. Their talent, patience, and insight are invaluable to me.

Nancy Clendaniel, an extraordinary photographer, came to Brightstar Farm and captured the life and the love of my farm on film. I will always treasure her intimate portraits of my animal family and recall the flawless, sunny summer day on which they were taken.

Original thinking is not a gift of mine. But I can take a good idea and share it, and this I do with gleeful abandon. My heartfelt thanks this year to Daniel Quinn, whose visionary writings renewed my hope for the world.

Relationships—with people and with animals—sustain and renew me like nothing else can, and the past few years have blessed me with so many good ones: Leslie and Vincent Mellott, new and precious extended family; Maureen Fredrickson, who loves ducks and chickens almost as much as I do; Sophie Craighead, who served as a one-woman marketing department for *Animals as Teachers and Healers*, giving away literally hundreds of copies of the book to friends; and Sharon Callahan, the first real-life angel I ever met. And to my neighbors in Troutdale, Oregon, a special thank-you for the richness of your lives and your stories, many of which fill these pages.

Because so much of my writing is a collection and assimilation of the stories of others, I am deeply beholden to readers' continuing contributions. Without these courageous and gentle tales, my work could not exist as it does. I am humbled and thankful that such personal stories have been entrusted to me. It is a delight to share them with a larger reading audience where they—and the animals they honor—will live and teach once again.

Lastly, loving acknowledgment to my cherished animal partners: Arrow, Strongheart, Mirella, Flora, Pumpkin, Polani, Aurora, and of course the fowl family.

Animals as Guides for the Soul

Teaching What We Most Want to Know

"In all things, even in the most recondite mysteries of the soul, nature is the first and finest of teachers."

—THOMAS MOORE

After the publication of my first book, *Animals as Teachers and Healers,* my publisher, Maureen Michelson, had an alarming dream about me. She told me that in her dream, I told her I would be dying soon. "What do you mean?" Maureen had replied to the dream me. "There is too much work you need to do! You can't be leaving now!"

Her dream came as no surprise to me. When I completed my first book, I felt as though my life's work was finished. In fact, I was so certain that I was done that I had begun to fear my life would end soon, probably with a recurrence of the cancer that had visited me ten years before. The way I saw it, if I had done what I'd been put on earth to do, why would I expect to stay around much longer? I found these thoughts bizarre and troublesome. As a first-time author, I had no idea that it is not unusual for a writer to feel utterly "finished" at the end of a book project. When Maureen told me about her dream, I admitted to her my feeling of being "all done" and confided that I couldn't possibly imagine what work I still needed to do.

Maureen said, "Your work is just beginning. Stick around and you'll see."

That was more than two years ago, and with hindsight I can say that we were both correct. In one sense, I *was* finished. The part of my life that existed before my book came into being died soon after the book reached the bookstores. Instead, I was reborn into a whole new life, one that demanded that I begin exploring more deeply the values I'd espoused in *Animals as Teachers and Healers*. In truth, my work *was* just beginning.

What I had committed to paper in my first book was the rough outline of a life-path: one nourished by contemplation of relationships other than human to human, a celebration of lessons learned at the four-footed threshold. In many ways, *Animals as Teachers and Healers* was my personal mission statement. Creating a mission statement is one thing. Living it is quite another.

In *Animals as Guides for the Soul*, I explore what it means to actually live a vision that acknowledges all living beings as gifted teachers and healers. Such an undertaking can be an enormous challenge in our obsessively human-focused culture. It is a commitment that enlists the soul.

By soul, I do not use the word in its religious dress. I have come to understand soul as the unseen, oftimes disowned inner guardian of our lives, a force weaving together the threads of heart, mind, and spirit that fashions us into an integrated piece of work. Thomas Moore describes the soul in this way: " 'Soul' is not a thing, but a quality of dimension of experiencing life and ourselves. It has to do with depth, value, relatedness, heart, and personal substance. . . . We know intuitively that soul has to do with genuineness and depth." Genuineness: This life quality surfaces repeatedly in my writing and in my life. To live in a manner that integrates conviction and action is to me the heart of a genuine life—a soul-full life.

Descartes said, "I think, therefore, I am." *That* I am has never seemed to me worth ruminating about. Of far greater consequence is *who* I am. Who I am is a woman who loves animals. This was not a choice, mind you. My enchantment with animals was a given from the moment I was born. My enchantment with animals dates back to before I could speak. My first stuttered word was *parakeet*. Psychologist James Hillman writes: "Sooner or later, something seems to call us onto a particular path. You may remember this 'something' as a signal moment in childhood when an urge struck out of nowhere, a fascination, a

peculiar turn of events struck like an annunciation: This is . . .
who I am." My soul spoke to me early in life about my connection to animals. I spent the next several decades, as many people
do, conveniently ignoring its wise voice.

My first book was a fresh acknowledgment of that soul's
whisper. The next task of my life, then, became twofold: First, to
see how fully I could live as a woman who loved animals. Then
to chart the emergence of other animal-oriented souls. Such a
collection of life stories would serve as guideposts to others on a
similar four-footed sojourn.

Although I am committed to living my life through an
animal-based philosophy, my experience makes one thing
abundantly clear: Nothing that happens between humans and
animals is separate from what happens in every other aspect
of human life. Who we are with animals mirrors who we are—
our fears, our joys, our dreams, our actions—in every other
arena of our lives. "Each species is a master of a particular way
of being that foreshadows something about ourselves," observes
human ecologist Paul Shepard. A commitment to living a
genuine life with animals cannot help but lead to richer human
relationships.

Why do I think of animals as guides for the soul? Because
love for animals is who I am. Each person has a unique passion
or soul-voice that cannot—must not—be denied. But for those
like me who have a deep affinity for animals, I believe animals

offer a particularly rich and rewarding track to personal awareness and to a more genuine and soul-filled life. Animals, for
example, do not allow us the luxury of complete and total projection. Unlike many other time-tested devotions such as theology, art, philosophy, or meditation, animals are living beings
with soul-lives of their own. They demand of us that we be
in relationship with them. They remain—for all our current
attempts to rid the world of many of them—in our faces.
Although we can effortlessly project our ideal fantasy selves
onto an evocative piece of writing, an inspired painting, or a religious icon, it is much harder to dismiss one's true nature in the
presence of, say, a spewed-up hairball on the floor, an attic full
of insulation-shredding raccoons, or the sixth pile of puppy
poop on one's white sofa.

Animals, in their blessed state of total presence, require our
presence as well. All animals possess the enviable quality of
complete acceptance of the moment—a quality some of us
meditate on for a lifetime, only to achieve in small measure.
Coming into animal presence, we may find ourselves refresh-
ingly alert to living in the moment.

Over the centuries, many animals have achieved archetypal
status, defining for us in their consistent purity of expression
certain states of being. Snakes reveal to us the secret of casting
off old life-skins for new ones. Crows and coyotes teach us the
power of foolery and folly. No living creature defines a life of

devotion and loyalty better than the dog. When we take the time to thoughtfully observe the lives of animals, these qualities speak to our spirits, inspire us, warn us, heal us.

In following an animal-inspired life-path, I find that the richest ground is often, coincidentally, the rockiest. Our relationships with animals are highly conflicted ones. "We adore them and we curse them. We caress them and we ravish them. We want them to acknowledge us and be with us. We want them to disappear and be autonomous. We abhor their viciousness and lack of pity, as we abhor our own viciousness and lack of pity. We love them and reproach them, just as we love and reproach ourselves," writes poet Pattiann Rogers. At the juncture of this conflict between humans and animals rests an enormous opportunity for self-revelation and growth. It is within the act of choosing where and how we will stand on this rough ground that our true spirit often reveals itself. When life plunges us into duality and confusion, the soul, whispering through the voice of our emotions, insights, symptoms, or dreams, encourages us to live in greater accord with what we value.

The challenges brought to my life by my animal family since the publication of my first book often feel like mine alone. However, if the hundreds of letters from my readers are any indication, these issues I claim as uniquely mine are shared by many: Is there a place in heaven for animals? Can we sometimes do a disservice to our animals in our exuberant efforts to communicate better with them? Do my dreams of animals mean anything? Why am I ashamed to share my joy of animals with other people? How can I better serve my animals, and is their service to me—to humankind—altruism or bondage? Is there healing for me in tragic events with animals— animals I am ashamed to say I have not served well? How can I help heal the relationship between humans and animals, between my animals and me?

These questions were the catalyst for *Animals as Guides for the Soul*. The themes they evoked became the five stations along the four-footed path explored in this book: spirituality, communication, service, forgiveness, and transformation. These are life issues common not only to animal lovers but to everyone.

Because I believe that home is where our soul work is most richly cultivated, the first chapter of this book is an intimate introduction to my home and animal family. This place, my farm called Brightstar, is the anchor point of my life and work, and we will return in story and experience to Brightstar and my animal family many times.

Next along the animal path is a journey into spirit. All of my life I have been in conflict with much of Western theology, which excludes or minimizes animals. To welcome animals back into my spiritual arena has required a revising of my personal theology. The qualities of enchantment, grace, and blessing can be treasure maps to a new, personally defined connection with the divine. Animals, in their otherness, beckon us into new modes of awareness and are adept at leading us to these three spiritual gold mines.

As a woman who twice nearly lost her voice to cancer, I have been struggling with issues of communication for a long time. Because communication is such an enormous and complex topic, I have devoted two chapters to its exploration. Chapter 2 discusses communication with animals on a direct level, while Chapter 3 celebrates communication of a more symbolic nature. This second realm of communicating embraces dreams, sudden insights, "messengers," angels, or "signs." Although we have been culturally indoctrinated to dismiss these means of ancient knowing, we would do well to tune our inner ears to these abandoned frequencies. Animals and animal images seem to thrive in this inner universe and can serve as gentle and surprising guides to alternative ways of wisdom.

Last year, I stumbled upon a quote that changed my life: "What is not given is lost." The truth of these few words becomes more evident to me every day, and their truth is particularly relevant to the theme of Chapter 4, service. Service is a critical station on the path to self-development and soulful living. But in my life, service has often been associated more with drudgery than with altruism. Animals have populated every real and imagined world of service, from the most ideal to the most tragic. Reflecting on animals' lives of ministry—and bondage—can bring us to a much deeper understanding of how service relates to feelings of freedom and imprisonment in our own lives.

Those who live most fully and most joyfully also know how to grieve. Yet culturally we are denied access to our grief. My former employer allowed three days of "grief leave" if an immediate family member died. Three days to do the work of years! Most difficult to mourn are the losses for which we feel responsible, actions of which we are ashamed. I remember striking my family dog repeatedly when I was very young. The memory, the shame, stings like icy rain forty years later. To forgive ourselves for our transgressions is the work of the soul. Because animals often suffer illness or accident or die in our care, they can serve as excellent missionaries to a place of reconciliation, healed grief, and forgiveness. Often, I believe animals come to our lives specifically to deliver this intimate gift, the awesome gift of their passing. Chapter 5 provides insight for reconciling these painful losses.

At a certain point in our personal development, we mature into a sense of reverence for the greater world. Enfolding the world into our circle of compassion, we recognize that the world needs healing as much as we do. Healing the relationship between humans and animals is crucial to restoring the health of the world. For many years, I have regarded my "enemies"— those who do not care for the world and for animals in the same manner that I do—with animosity. Upon reflection, I have observed that bitterness and hate are qualities I never witness in the animal kingdom. The antelope does not hate the wolf. Animals instruct me to put aside judgment, lick a wound whether it be mine or another's, give thanks for life, and make room for others at the manger. This is how the healing of the world begins, and how those committed to this transformation can go forward. The final chapter of *Animals as Guides for the Soul* explores the nature of peace, of vision, and of transformation. Although the focus of this chapter is on transforming the relationship between humans and animals, the methods I suggest are universal in their application: stimulate transformation in one place and you initiate transformation in other places as well.

To travel along this five-stationed animal path to the soul, I have used the vehicle of story. When I had cancer, I learned quickly that stories were far more healing to me than statistics or information. Although stories are still frequently disparaged as anecdotal evidence in some professional circles, the winds are changing. Physician Rachel Naomi Remen "doctors" with the use of stories—telling them, listening to them. Dean Ornish, M.D., writes: "There is no meaning in facts. As a physician and a human being, I live in a world of stories. . . . Stories are the language of community." Ornish also reminds us that if good information and facts were all it took to change human behavior, "no one would smoke"! Thomas Moore advises, "Stories offer a powerful way for the soul to find a space for itself."

Everyone's story is unique, yet all stories are the one story of our humanness. Not surprisingly, stories that tell of the lives of animals often seem universal as well, as though we can see the light of our dog's eyes in every creature's eyes. If we look with an unprejudiced heart, we may see our own eyes reflected in every creature's eyes, as well.

Real stories do not usually have tidy endings, or indeed, any endings. Many of the stories told in this book leave just as much untold. Animals enter, dwell for a time, leave, and become memories or dreams. Human companions are left to weave the meaning of the encounter into their hearts. As such, this is not a book of answers. It is instead an intimate exploration of issues that face us all: issues of relationship, integrity, conflict, and reconciliation, all told in the mythic form of story. All of these stories star an animal, a memory of an animal, a dream of an animal.

Each chapter ends in a story—one or two of my own and one or more from readers. These stories, some subtle and some dramatic, embody part of the essence of that chapter. Several are stories that reveal decades of accumulated life-experience.

It is my fervent hope that in reading these animal stories, both mine and others, you will be inspired to share your own.

The world is hungry for stories that affirm the deep affinity between humans and animals. All of our stories—those that ended well and even those that ended with more confusion than we would have liked—offer great hope to a world longing to heal the relationship between animals and humans.

—SUSAN CHERNAK MCELROY
Brightstar Farm

CHAPTER ONE

Brightstar Farm: Between Two Rivers

> "Some spirits are stronger than others, says al-Kindi. The farm spirit is one of the strong ones, the needed ones."
>
> —THOMAS MOORE,
> *The Re-Enchantment of Everyday Life*

"Shush, Bear, shush now. It's over. We're here." In the backseat cat carrier, Bear momentarily ceased the piteous meowing he had begun in Washington and maintained all the way down the coast to Northwest Oregon. Flora and Evinrude, packed in beside him, had not uttered a sound in three hours. Arrow, my shepherd/collie puppy, crawled into my lap and yawned as I turned into the gravel driveway. The house in front of us, a small, red thing older than I was, sat empty in the snowstorm that had begun on Christmas, the day before. Snowdrifts banked up along the garage and blanketed the uncovered brick porch. The house was ours, our new home. The first home I had ever owned in my life.

Our decision to leave Bainbridge Island was career based. My husband, Lee, had been offered a promising job in Oregon, and I pushed him to accept it. After one day of searching, we had found this little house, made a quick offer, and were packed and moving a month later. For what I'd given up—the island, our friends and family, and the beauty of Puget Sound—I got our first house and some tantalizing possibilities. For behind the house, which was uncommonly characterless for such an old place, lay an acre of ground with outbuildings, trees, fences, and an old barn. In front of the house across the narrow country road was an eighty-acre cow pasture that opened green arms to a breathtaking view of farms, fields, timber-covered hills, and river country. Off to the left up the street, Mount Hood poked out white and startling behind a windbreak of huge old syca-mores. A tiny stretch of the Columbia River was visible over the cedar hedge in our backyard, and the Sandy River stretched like a twisting silver salmon at the foot of our hill. We sat between two rivers on the crest of the Columbia River Gorge, a national scenic area.

Still, enthusiasm didn't come to me easily there in the driveway that first day with a car full of anxious animals and a demanding wind that rattled the car and whipped the snow-drifts into white veils. The Columbia Gorge is called the windsurfing capital of the world for good reason. I had noticed that all the trees in the area had stunted, tired-looking branches on their east-facing sides, but I didn't consider what that might really mean until that afternoon in the driveway. In the years to come, that wind would mean ice storms and trees falling and painfully cold ears. It would mean canceling walks around the block until spring, when the winds relaxed enough to allow you to stand upright on the road. And it would mean nights when the wind shook the windows, moaning, and hurled tree limbs and ice clumps against the side of the house.

I picked up the king-sized cat carrier in the backseat, grabbed the end of Arrow's leash, and hurried into the house and out of the winter wind. Thirty years of living had been removed since I'd last seen the place almost two months before. The harvest-gold shag carpets were threadbare, just cleaned, and still wet. The basement was dark, hollow-sounding, and forbidding. In the kitchen, the three colors of ancient Formica countertop were dusty and littered with old breakfast crumbs. When I released the cats from the carrier, they burst into the room and headed, as cats do, to the edges of the rooms. All three immediately began snaking their way nose-first along the baseboards. Arrow trotted to the back door and I let her out. Across the lawn she raced, making dizzying circles of fresh tracks, burrowing her nose deep into the cold snow, then sneezing in explosive fits. Wind grabbed her long coat and turned it to dancing brown fire.

Soon Lee would arrive with the rented van. But these first few hours in our new home were mine to savor with our small family of animals. Pulling the cat carrier over by the back sliding door, I sat on it and watched Arrow dance in the falling, swirling snow. Silently I waited, feeling the promise of that vacant house between two rivers. As I watched Arrow in her joy, I knew that coming to this house and this land was a turning point for me. Much of my life had been spent in apartments and suburbs, with the drone of traffic never far away. Street-lights blocked out the dark of night and the brightness of the stars. My animals were often "illegal renters," sneaked in and hidden away from less-than-tolerant landlords.

Sitting by the wide-open back door, I took in great, deep breaths of cold air. I had always dreamed of myself in a place like this, yet I would come to see that my imaginings had been cramped and tiny in comparison with the fullness of my life in this house. In the four years to come, this house would witness my grief at the death of my father, foster the conception of two books, see the birthing of donkey babies and scores of chicks and ducklings, and offer shelter to countless lost and hurt animals. Friendships would be born, nurtured, and lost here. Precious animal companions would die, their bodies given over to the deep soil of this place. I would rediscover the moon on summer nights. And the wind and I would become tentative friends.

That afternoon as I watched the cats weave in and out of

the vacant rooms, I couldn't know that I was stepping deep into the school of country life. These grounds would become home, and some of my greatest lessons would come from the teachers who would soon share this acre with me.

THE BARN

Because the winter had been so hard, the former owners had not been able to fully remove thirty years of living before our move-in date. The barn out in the back pasture was still bulging with their belongings when we arrived: an old truck, a loft crammed with boxes and antique furniture, some stall boards, bulky farm machinery that I could not identify, a fifty-gallon drum of lime, a motorcycle, old batteries, amorphous heaps of who-knew-what—all of it covered with thick layers of dusty cob-webbing. The hillside between the barn and our house was littered with stacks of old glass windows, mounds of truck tires, broken bricks, rag piles, a burn site, and several moldy camper shells.

For several months, the weather remained fierce and the yard far too wet to handle the weight of moving vehicles. And so from December on, I looked out of my kitchen window toward the gloom of winter pastures and a hillside dressed with wet junk. Weather kept everyone indoors. No children played on the country road. No neighbors visited across winter frozen fences.

A couple of times that season, I went poking around the barn. Built with ancient wood from an abandoned homestead, the barn was an imposing old red building with a small wooden steeple on top and heavy, sliding doors. It stood sure and silent and eternal against the east winds. Trees surrounded it, swinging their branches low to rake the tin roof. A lean-to was nailed on the south side, and I could tell by the old tire tracks leading to it that it had served as a garage for most of its life.

The notion of having my very own barn was enchanting. Since my childhood, I have dreamed of having a barn of my own. Now I had a barn, yet this barn set my very teeth on edge. It was not warm and inviting, filled with animal smells and straw bales. Something about the building, looming out there in the pasture like the Addams Family Mansion, made my skin crawl. Inside, the ancient, sheet-covered furniture looked as though it belonged to an old ghost, and the hulking farm truck was a monster. There was no sound in the barn save the endless droning of the hard, winter wind and the fingernail scraping of tree branches across the roof. Looking into the barn, I felt like an unwelcome intruder. After two unsettling visits, I stayed far away from that part of the yard for the rest of the winter.

One morning in early March, trucks pulled into the driveway and an assortment of workers, one of them the previous owner, began hauling things off the hillside and out of the barn. For the next six days they worked, and I watched the piles of glass and bricks on the hillside slowly disappear. When they were done, the hillside was bare dirt. The barn doors were ajar.

Early the next morning, before the birds were even up, I put on a jacket and hat and walked hesitantly toward the barnyard. From under the thick shelter of the Douglas firs, a crow suddenly exploded into flight, careening past my face with a sweep of black feathers and a harsh scream. Startled, I froze under the canopy of branches. Around me, other birds began to move, awakened by the crow. Wings rustled and I heard questioning chirps. Several small birds flew out into the morning.

After taking a few deep breaths, I continued through the pasture. When I peeked inside the door of the barn, I saw the dirt floor stretched out bare and hard. For the first time, I could see the barn walls: strips of wood painted a hundred years ago in now-faded pastel. The loft was nearly empty; only a few old bales of hay remained. Mangers and stall gates and a rickety blue ladder had been left behind, propped up by the door. I grabbed the ladder and quickly climbed up into the loft, looking down at the quiet expanse of empty building. For the first time, I could hear the sounds of the barn itself. The stillness of the air, the motion of a small creature in the hay, the whisper of morning mist on the roof. A thin slice of light poked a dusty finger through a crack high up in the wall. In the rafters, I saw old summer nests of wasps and swallows. The smell of dust and hay rose up all around me.

Eyes closed, I breathed in the sweet particular scent of this place. My uneasiness surrendered to enchantment. This was the barn I had dreamed of since my girlhood. A magic, spirit-filled place, like a cathedral, holding old secrets, old dreams, old memories of animals that had been born, lived, and died within its walls. Our farmhouse had been transformed into my creation, filled with my smells, my furniture, my music, but the barn held a life of its very own. I had transformed the house, but the barn, I knew, would transform me.

Carefully, reverently, I climbed down the ladder to the dirt floor. In the lean-to, I found a shredded old broom and began sweeping the barn walls with deliberate and firm strokes, clearing away the great hanging cobwebs and lifetimes of dust. I swept the loft and moved the mangers into corners. Soon, I hoped, animals would be eating from them. Finally I carried in a hose, baptized the walls and rafters, and swept the water off of the hard-packed earth floor. Then I stopped and waited, and listened for something. Nothing came.

Outside, I wiped my hands on my jeans. In the cool of the late spring morning, I felt renewed and refreshed. The barn was reclaimed, consecrated, hallowed. Now I could sit in its loft and listen to its whisperings, and it to mine. As I walked back toward the house, a nursery rhyme I chanted as a child filled my thoughts: *Star light, star bright, first star I see tonight. Wish I may, wish I might* ... And I named our farm Brightstar.

THE FAMILY

The heavy wooden manger waiting in one corner of the barn was an invitation I couldn't resist. I was aching to expand our animal family. So on April 10, we slapped up a temporary stall and brought home Guido, a tiny miniature donkey with legs like tree stumps and a butt like a locomotive. Guido was small, but he was built to last. At six months of age, he was a solid brick of energy and character. We were so enamored with him that we had three more mini-donkeys ensconced in the pasture by that fall. The three donkeys became ten by the end of the following summer. The donkeys—resolute, patient, and each with its unique ear-rattling bray—quickly became the soul of our farm. Chicks and ducks of every color and kind arrived in a cardboard box from the feed store in May. They lived in our kitchen for two weeks before we made some modifications to the greenhouse and christened it an official henhouse. Soon the sound of roosters was competing with the hee-hawing of the donkeys.

The following summer, Phaedra the llama moved in and kept good company with the donkeys. Her gentle nature was so complete that she never once spit green gunk at her pasture mates, who more than deserved it on many occasions. Phaedra's alfalfa and special diet pellets were forbidden fruit to the donkey herd, but they managed on occasion to sneak into her stall, calmly butt Phaedra out of the way, and inhale her dinner while she looked over their heads and hummed the characteristic soft hum of llamas in quiet resignation.

Cats just seemed to appear and disappear over the coming years, some taking residence in the barn before finding the magic path to the cat door and the house. Arrow learned to live with cats of every color and stripe, and was gracious and welcoming. Her patience amazed me, since it seemed that she was always bearing kitty scratches on her long collie nose. Flora, the tuxedo cat who had beaten feline leukemia as a kitten; Evinrude, the huge, ultra-relaxed tiger tom who came to us with a purr like a boat engine; and Mirella, a feral barn cat who took to the high life of house living as though the place was built for her, formed the permanent trio. Evinrude and Mirella kept the house free of shrews, mice, and voles. Flora's prey of choice has always been bugs, and she is by far the best fly catcher—and only fly eater—in the house.

Caruso, the canary, came to live with us and filled winter and summer months with the sweetest and most passionate music I've ever heard before or since. Tristan and Isolde, an intense pair of geese who took no prisoners in their guardianship of the yard, moved in with Phaedra, Guido, and the rest of the donkey clan. Not a single chicken so much as stuck a questioning claw in the barnyard during the geese's brief but magnificent reign. A cougar carried Isolde off the following year, leaving nothing but a bloodied heart behind. I gave Tristan to a friend with a lonely white female goose, knowing that I was helpless to fully protect him from the fate that had taken his beloved Isolde.

Most of these animals—let's be honest here: all of these animals—were my idea. I found them, fell in love with them, and welcomed them into our growing family. Lee cherished most of our animal family members, accepted some, and tolerated others. Tristan and Lee had an especially horrid relationship. Though Tristan bears no scars from their encounters, Lee can show you several. So it was with utter amazement that I watched Lee sell his cherished Rolex watch—a status symbol of his young manhood—to bring home Pumpkin, a magnificent and high-priced Moluccan cockatoo. Lee rolled her cage into our living room late one evening, fresh from the pet store, with absolute giddy delight. From inside the immense, blanketed stainless-steel birdcage, I heard a soft "Uh, hello . . . Helloooh?" A large beak the color of gray slate poked from beneath the cage covering. "I'm a pretty, pretty giiirrrrl," Pumpkin advised us. Suddenly I understood why the Rolex got sold.

THE HOUSE, the barn, our animal family—these became the ingredients for my continuing quest for a greater healing and for greater intimacy with all beings. Questions about my life, about animals, and about my beliefs took form on walks to and from the barn. I weathered nights of disappointment, grief, and shame beneath the gentle caress of sheltering firs and icy stars. Surrounded by my loving family of animals, I found nurturance, patience, and a measure of peace. So here the stories unfold. At Brightstar Farm. My home between two rivers.

CHAPTER TWO

A Blessing from the Animals

"I think it was from the animals that Saint Francis learned it is possible to cast yourself on the earth's good mercy and live."

—JANE HIRSHFIELD

When I was quite young, maybe nine or ten, I first heard about the religious tradition of the Blessing of the Animals. The idea of animals in church made instant sense. Animals were a delightful mystery to me, just as God was a mystery to me, so I always partnered animals and God in my mind. I imagined how wonderful it must be to enter a church and be welcomed by a family of animals! And how much more wonderful to be blessed by them! In my childhood fantasy, I saw the animals waiting regally at the altar. Animals of every color and type—giraffes, dogs, an elephant, a lion or a zebra, maybe even a frog—all gathered at the pulpit, waiting to bestow a special blessing on the human congregation. Never did it occur to me that in this religious tradition the animals were to *receive* a blessing rather than to bestow one. When my mother explained to me that this was the case, that it was the animals who were to be blessed, I was terribly disappointed. Why, I wondered, would animals ever need our blessing? I liked my idea much better.

As a middle-aged adult, I'm still asking myself that question. It seems absurd that humans would presume to bless animals. In *Natural Grace*, former Dominican priest Matthew Fox writes, "I've always been repelled by the notion that animals need our blessing. Animals don't need our blessing, we need their blessing. It should be a blessing *from* the animals—that would be the real praise."

When I speak about my relationship with animals, I often think of the words *grace* and *blessing*. These evocative words elicit a myriad of images and feelings unique to each person; however, many of us use these words in a spiritual context. Searching for definitions of grace and blessing that ring true for me, I find Fox's definition closest to my own experience: "Grace is about gift. Grace is unconditional love. Grace, therefore, is about blessing, because blessing is the theological word for *goodness*, and a gift is presumably something good. . . . Creation is *grace*. And we didn't do it. It was someone else setting the table for us."

As embodiments of grace and blessing, animals have been setting the table for me all my life. They serve as my doorway to particular states of mind and heart that I reach most easily and consistently in their presence. Some of the richest blessings my animal family brings to me are those of joy, enchantment, magic, mystery, and authenticity. My stories of the blessings of animals are simple ones, yet their impact on my life is immense. Dozens of ordinary animal-centered vignettes fill my days. These moments could easily go unnoticed in the course of a too-busy day. But when I pause for just an instant and bask in the delight of these moments, I am suddenly transported to an enchanted world where I feel nourished and comforted.

My midlife has been marked with bouts of mild to severe depression. I'm not talking about an extended case of the blues, but about protracted periods of emotional deadness that have required medication to alleviate. I live in the Pacific Northwest, where gray winters can make the shadow of depression seem even darker and longer. Some mornings I wake up and find little reason to get out of bed, except to let out the chickens and feed the animals at Brightstar Farm.

Recently I had such a morning. I awoke to the drumming of rain on the porch roof and clouds like lumps of wet coal. The ground was saturated, moving beneath my feet like pudding. Last fall's leaves, mounds of them I'd never gotten around to raking up, were slowly decomposing in the driveway and along the paths to the barn, slick as ice and black with rot. As usual, the east wind raged out of the back pasture and hit my face with hands of stinging cold.

I felt just like the rain: sodden, shapeless, splattering down. My first stop was the chicken house. One of our hens surprised me with a tiny chick she had hatched secretly in the barn loft. Gray as a cloud, soft as a wisp of smoke, and not much bigger than a Q-tip, the chick was a lively antidote to the foreboding dark of that winter morning. I listened to its sweet, muffled peeps, which sounded confident and rich with life and promise. I don't remember how long I sat there admiring the newest member of our chicken family. In the new-life world of the henhouse, the rain seemed far away and the wind nothing but a sweet breeze.

After I had secured the hen and her chick in a small protective pen, I headed to the barn to feed the donkeys. Stepping into a barn is like stepping into another world. The smells of hay, manure, and dust mark this peaceful home of my barn animals. On the lid of the grain bin were perfectly preserved little mud prints with telltale thumb markings—the calling card of Ever Vigilant, our resident wild raccoon. I traced my finger along the outline of the prints, remembering when Arrow had last run him up the maple tree in the yard—a regular summer-evening event. And in that moment, despite the wintry day, I could smell the cut grass of summer and hear the rustle of green maple leaves.

Behind me, our ducks, Geronimo and Crazy Horse, dabbled in the mud puddle at the barn door, chattering intensely, spraying dirty water up the back of my pant leg. The donkeys were delighted to see me. Guinness thrust his brown, satiny nose into my hands, eager for rubs. Polani noogied my leg and flapped me with ears the size of French bread loaves. Aurora lined up in front of me, fanny first, waiting for her butt scratches. Surrounded by all the milling, nuzzling, hay-nibbling contentment expressed by my family in the barn, I began to feel a sweet appreciation for life tickling at the corners of my dark mood.

When I returned to the house, after one more stop at the henhouse to enjoy the new chick, I felt much less like melting back into bed. So I fetched Pumpkin, our cockatoo, from her cage for a morning shower. Pumpkin showers with me several times a week to keep her feathers in good shape. She always seems to enjoy a long, warm rinse, but this morning she was particularly enthused. Normally during her shower time, Pumpkin is quiet and reflective, moving her shoulders back and forth a bit to move the water over her pale pink feathering. Not this morning. She began bobbing her head side to side and chattering excitedly as we entered the shower. As soon as the spray of water touched her, she spread her wings and dipped and twirled them in circles like a magnificent peach-tinted cape. Her tail lifted and spread into an exquisite fan. She stretched her neck out and fluffed her salmon crest and began giggling loudly, spraying diamond-colored droplets of water with her wings and tail. Her mouth was open, her eyes squeezed shut in glee. First one reptilian foot, then the other lifted in an avian two-step. I felt as if I were holding a huge ball of peach-colored light, and that the light was dancing in my hands. Throughout her shower, Pumpkin danced and laughed, stopping only when I at last turned off the water.

When we stepped from the shower, the last vestige of gray was gone from my morning. And gone for the time being was my cloud of depression. All I needed was a good dose of enchantment, and my animal family had obliged. Thomas Moore wrote an entire book on the value of enchantment, *The Re-Enchantment of Everyday Life*. He writes:

> Enchantment is a spell that comes over us, an aura of fantasy and emotion that can settle on the heart. . . . An enchanted life has many moments when the heart is overwhelmed by beauty and the imagination is electrified by some haunting quality in the world or by a spirit or voice speaking from deep within a thing, a place, or a person. The soul has an absolute, unforgiving need for regular excursions into enchantment. It requires them like the body needs food and the mind needs thought.

Animals are exceptional purveyors of enchantment and charm. When I am in the company of animals I find myself deliciously transported out of the hectic world of modern human existence and into a luminous landscape of wonder and possibility. Animals help me feel my deep connection to the earth. Some people find their enchantment in music, art, dance, religion, or writing. I find it in nature and in animals, and in my home that welcomes the energies of both.

Last summer, the day before we were to leave for a week's vacation, we took Pumpkin to stay with a friend who was delighted to care for her in our absence. That night, as we sat in our Pumpkin-less living room, we realized just how great a spell Pumpkin had cast on our home in her brief year with us. The very walls seemed dull and lifeless without her animated nightly antics. Arrow, our dog, sighed heavily throughout the evening. So did we.

For animals to bring us to the doorway of enchantment does not require miracles or feats of great effort. I have seen Arrow transform an office into a magic village with nothing more than her presence. Arrow is a loving, sociable dog whose greatest delight in life is greeting people with the same level of enthusiasm she bestows on meaty bones and dog cookies. Because Arrow is a certified therapy dog in the state of Oregon, where she has been specially trained to work in hospital, conva-lescent, and therapeutic settings, she is allowed access where most animals, sadly, are not. I take her on shopping trips and often take her traveling with me. It seems that the more artifi-cial the environment—the more plastic, glass, concrete, and imitation plants—the more effective Arrow's presence is. She can turn an elevator of strangers into a group of smiling, chatting, "old friends" in less than six floors. Any room she graces becomes an instant Mecca of goodwill, happy faces, and workers rolling around on the floor for a therapeutic dog kiss and hug. She mesmerizes children in grocery stores, gets perfect strangers to tell each other their favorite animal stories in the checkout lines, and stops animated conversations midsentence as people blurt out, "Hey, just a moment! Can I pet that dog?"

It used to annoy me that Arrow and I could rarely walk fifty feet without someone approaching us with questions or asking to pet her, but then I realized that Arrow's true therapy work has nothing to do with her certification. She weaves magic spells spontaneously. Now, when strangers ask to visit with Arrow, I usually encourage them because I know what a kiss from a friendly dog can do for the soul. Arrow is an ambassador; I'm just her escort. Many animals can affect people this way. At my previous job, my manager once brought her rabbit to work. The rabbit completely charmed the office all day long as workers lined up for their "rabbit fix." Everyone was happier and more generous in spirit because of the rabbit's gentle presence.

Workplaces can be hard environments to brighten up. Priscilla Thomas wrote me about a wild bird who transformed her day in a difficult job situation:

A few years ago, I was working in an impoverished environment in a converted Quonset hut. A glass "cage" constructed inside the hut housed the office staff. The air was stuffy and hot, the work conditions were primeval, with a buzzer sounding for a ten-minute coffee break in the morning and in the afternoon. One joyless late afternoon when I opened the door to my little glass cubicle, I discovered a bird flying about in great distress. The manager of the office ran in, hoping to extricate the little creature by capturing it. Unable to stand there watching while the bird frantically hit one glass wall after another, I urged the manager to leave and let me deal with the bird, which he gladly did. I stood silently in the cubicle for some time. Then I said to the bird in as calm a voice as I could manage, "I don't know how I'm going to get you out of here, but I *will* get you out." The bird cocked its head in comprehension, and as I walked slowly toward it, it flew to the top of my head and landed there. For moments I stood motionless, bird on my head. Then I understood that the bird was trying to give me a message. So we walked through the office, down a corridor, out several doors, and into the sunshine. Only then did the bird fly off my head to freedom.

The experience was a significant spiritual moment. The bird seemed to have walked me through the tedium of that environment, and the remainder of my time spent there became significant. Many of the staff opened up to me, the "bird lady," showing their lighter and more gentle selves. My attitude changed about the nature of the work. I felt touched. Later on, I learned that the event with the bird had occurred on Saint Francis's birthday.

Each day I realize anew the importance of things that can take us out of our daily, life-draining busyness and transport us for a moment into a numinous, enchanted reality where our souls can renew themselves. Recently I was honored to speak before an auditorium of cancer survivors, and I told them about my little cat Flora, who had survived feline leukemia. I told them that Flora had taught me that healing could be about joy. And that for me, joy was a major component in my own healing from cancer. Later that evening, to my delighted surprise, Carl Simonton, M.D., world-renowned oncologist and a healing visionary, also spoke to the assembly about joy. "As a cellular biologist, I can see every moment of joy, ecstasy, and delight written in each cell of your body. And I can also see each moment of despair, hopelessness, and defeat." He spoke of the courage it takes to find and follow joy in life, and how each person's joy is different. Joy, he said, is a cornerstone of healing.

When I lose my way and need to be reminded of what joy feels like, what it looks like, I turn to the animals. For me, no greater embodiments of unfettered joy exist. Many of us lose our precious link with life's exuberance when we leave childhood, and that is a tragedy. We were not meant to put these riches away. Joy can be a barometer for how fully we are living our lives.

Unfortunately, most people go to great lengths to avoid joy. The late Danaan Parry, international peacemaker and counselor, wrote that people run away from moments of joy because these can be moments of great intensity. Parry believed that intensity is something we are taught to avoid at all costs, and that strong feelings of any kind are not encouraged in our society. In his book *Warriors of the Heart*, Parry wrote about an enlightening lesson of joy delivered to him by a school of wild dolphins he encountered in Mexico. The dolphins appeared alongside his small sailboat one afternoon, and Parry slipped overboard to be with them in the crystal blue waters of Baja. Frolicking and playing with the dolphins, Parry wrote that he was as close to ecstasy as he could imagine when a voice in his head said, "Be with us, Danaan." The phrase kept repeating itself until he realized it was a message from the dolphins. "I *am* with you." He laughed delightedly. "Be with us, Danaan," they repeated. In a sudden bolt of insight, he realized that even though he was reveling in the ecstatic joy of the moment, a part of him was diluting the experience by thinking about all the terrible things people had done to dolphins throughout history. So he took a leap of faith, put the thoughts aside, and did what the dolphins asked. He was *with* them 100 percent. Danaan's success as a peacemaker was fully dependent upon his willingness to be completely present in every conflict situation. The more he could stay focused on the moment, the more effective he was.

It is especially tempting to dismiss our joy about animals because animals are given so little honor in our world. In turn, emotions about animals are considered childish and are often denigrated. But if one of your greatest joys is animals, trust that joy. Romp with animals, fuss over them, be silly for them, and indulge yourself in their lives. Regardless of what others may say about your "eccentricities," remember that critics will never heal you. There is great power in joy and great healing in being who you really are. If you can't remember what joy looks like, spend more time watching animals. Not zoo animals—you will see little joy there—but companion animals and wild animals. Watch a cat in the sun. Spend time feeding ducks at a lake. Take a dog for a brisk walk and let him stop to sniff each piece of mysterious, delectable sidewalk gunk. Watch a hummingbird on a spring flower. Sit quietly by a stream and watch for streaks of silver on a fish's back. Listen in the dark on a moonless night for the conversations of owls and frogs. Breathe in all the joy that greets you in any given moment. It is a blessing and a healing.

I exchanged letters and "baby" pictures of Pumpkin with a wonderful medical doctor who credited his birds with bringing great joy into his life: "Most of my life has been in the shadows of depression, sometimes quite profound. But now I rise and see the antics and comedic intelligence of the birds I look after (or really, who look after me) and find, absolutely miraculously, that within a few minutes each morning I am laughing and being thankful to start another day. Although I was raised to appreciate the phrase *Physician, heal thyself*, and while I have been (hopefully) a good healer for over twenty years, it is now clear that animals have been my healers."

One reader, Rita Rizzo, wrote that the greatest gift of her new puppy is joy, and coincidentally, that is what she named her new friend: "Her name sums up all we have received from her and from all the wonderful animals whose lives we have shared. A friend began collecting Joy quotes, and my favorite is by Leon Bloy: 'Joy is the most infallible sign of the presence of God.' "

AUTHENTICITY IS A VALUABLE BLESSING from animals. None of us likes phonies, yet many of us don't quite know how to be—to quote my mother-in-law—"realies." My donkeys offer an especially vivid example of what a genuine life—no apologies—looks like. Donkeys do what they want when they want. They are not interested in your timetable or your agenda. Some call this kind of behavior stubborn. I prefer to call my donkeys "resolute of purpose." They study new things closely: a new lead rope, a new wheelbarrow, a new fence post. They accept new things into their environment only after careful, meditative reflection. If I try to rush them into anything, they swivel their ears and quiver their whiskered lower lips. Feet planted like boulders against my insistent tugs or shoves, they heave heavy disgusted sighs, as if to say, "Why have you so little patience, so little sense of proper timing?" It took me a week to convince Polani to enter our new horse trailer willingly. Once in, however, she decided for herself that it was a safe place. Now she never hesitates to load. Most times, she's in the trailer before I manage to get a halter on her.

Once a donkey gets something, it is got, and that is that. They are just that way. And they seem to do just fine taking life at their own honest pace. I take heart living with donkeys. If they can be who they are and get along in life, maybe there is room in the world for me, too. Maybe I can move at my own pace, with my own idiosyncrasies, and be welcomed in the world. My vow to myself since my bout with cancer ten years ago has been to take the time to lead the most authentic, genuine life I can. Like many women, I grew up learning how to adapt to others. It's only been in my midlife that I've begun exploring the notion of being myself. Animals serve as excellent examples of authenticity and integrity. They show me what being true to one's self really looks like, including honoring your own timeline.

MY ANIMAL FAMILY has blessed me by showing me doorways to lives that I will never live. I explore these lifetimes vicariously with animals. I have never had children, yet motherhood is a path I am led down each spring at Brightstar Farm by my donkeys, my hens, and the wild birds that nest in our yard. In each miraculous birth, each moment of fragile infancy and mother love, I see sterling examples of the universal goddess or feminine energy in action in the animal kingdom. Sometimes I actually feel the swell of motherhood in my own breast as I experience these tender examples of mother and child in the barn, the henhouse, and nests cradled in the trees.

One spring evening several years ago, I moved a sleeping bag into the barn loft and kept an all-night vigil with Sisi, a pregnant donkey waiting to birth her first foal. At first the hours passed slowly. Sisi paced and sweated in her hay-filled foaling stall as I leaned anxiously over the ledge of the loft, whispering continuous encouragement. Sometime during the night I felt a shift inside me, a letting go, and my entire world became that barn and the night in a timeless, hay-sweet capsule. Enfolded in the soft amber circle of a heat lamp, Sisi and I exchanged long looks. From the loft, I watched as her sides heaved and twisted with the labored turning of her foal.

At one point, Sisi gazed up at me with eyes that seemed to say, *Watch, this is how life comes. Like this . . .* I stumbled down the ladder with towels and a bucket and rubbed her shaking, wet flanks. Glancing outside, I wondered how much time had passed? Hours? The wind raced through the trees, and I could see long shadows of moonlight reaching through the pasture. Suddenly there was a gush of hot water on my pant legs as Sisi's water broke. Then she was on her side, pushing and groaning. Her fig-sized vagina had opened to the size of a small melon, and from its pink interior poked a tiny hoof, and then another. With each contraction and push, the hooves would extend, then disappear back inside of her. This went on for what I instinctively sensed was too long. Sisi looked exhausted. So I settled down behind her and placed both of Sisi's back feet against my breastbone. I grasped the small protruding hooves and called out to her, "Sisi, please push for me ... now." She groaned and braced her feet against me and pushed. Suddenly, miraculously, there was a wet bundle of broomstick legs and floppy ears struggling in my arms. The thick rope of umbilical chord stretched out along my leg and I could feel its pulse of life beating against my shin. How much time had passed?

Sisi raised her head and nickered to her infant. I lifted him up and placed him by her side, leaning back just in time to feel a steaming mass of afterbirth slide onto my lap. Lifting the placenta in my hands, I felt the membranes ooze between my fingers and smelled the pungent, warm aroma of blood and birth. For a moment, I held the mystery of birth and life.

Under the ethereal glow of the heat lamp, I cleaned up and lingered long enough to watch Starry Knight find his first meal at Sisi's teats. On the way back to the house under a dawning sky, I pressed my hands to my belly and said a silent prayer for the blessing of *my* first birth. These moments are as close to motherhood as I will ever come, and I thank my animal family for the grace of them.

ANIMALS CAN BLESS US by anointing us. This is the phrase I use to describe that delicious sensation of being singled out or acknowledged by an animal. When I was small, I took great delight in being the only person able to approach the wild cats in our alley. They were the kings and queens of the street, and I felt honored to be "received" by them. This sense of being singled out or anointed by a special animal is a well-kept special feeling of many animal lovers.

A friend visited with us for a couple of days and met our cockatoo for the first time. Pumpkin is a little reserved around strangers and takes a few days to settle in with visitors. On the second day, Pumpkin began tentatively chatting with my friend and then did her the royal honor of bowing her head and asking for some head rubs. As she bent over Pumpkin's perch to oblige, I heard her whisper, "Oh, thank you!" And I knew exactly how she felt. She had been anointed by our cockatoo.

A man named Donald told me about a wild young colt called Cuervo who lived on his grandfather's farm many years ago. No one could approach the beautiful, exuberant young animal, yet when Donald came to the farm, Cuervo wouldn't leave him alone and would actually jump fences just to follow and nuzzle the young boy. "I was a geeky kid, clumsy, not special in any way, but to have that horse take such notice of me— well, I stepped a lot prouder. What did he see in me? I couldn't imagine, but it must have been something wonderful to elicit that kind of a response. The family talked about it all the time, and I soaked up the attention like a sponge. When I became a teenager and felt especially lost and out of place, I'd think about Cuervo and I'd stand taller."

ONE OF THE MOST IMPORTANT WAYS that animals have blessed me has been in showing me a path to my own spirituality. I was raised in a Christian household. For decades I struggled with the notion of a God who was the embodiment of pure love and absolute judgment—two notions that never seemed harmonious to me. The Bible said that I was born in God's image and that the earth and all its inhabitants were under my "dominion." In church, I learned that I was blessed with a soul, while animals were not. In the Bible, animals were sacrificed, and yet Jesus said, "Inasmuch as ye have done it unto one of the least of these my brethren, ye have done it unto me." The contradictions baffled me. When my first animal companion, a lively hooded rat named Louie, died in my hands when I was eight years old, I simply could not conceive that so gentle a soul would find no home in heaven. I asked myself, "How could God have no place at his side for such a wondrous companion as Louie the rat?"

By the time I was a teenager, the notion that humans were God's chosen children and the rest of creation was below us was deeply unsettling. At that time, I was surrounded by a magnificent family of animals: our dog, Lady; my pet snakes; squirrels; a kangaroo rat; our cat, Boots; and a mockingbird foundling. All of these creatures welcomed me into their circle of friendship, trusted me, spoke to me. How could I bear the loneliness of human existence without their encouraging, loving presence at my side as equals and partners in the community of life? My spiritual upbringing, which I was told would be a source of comfort, solace, and courage, became instead my shame. I would not acknowledge any chosen status if my animals would not be chosen too, and so I grew wary and suspicious of God. By my early thirties, I did not like God very much at all.

In her book *The Origin of Satan*, Elaine Pagels, a professor of religion at Princeton University, notes that the translation of the Greek word for heresy means choice, and a heretic is "one who makes a choice." Originally, heretics were considered people who asked questions, who questioned the consensus. By Pagels's definition, I would consider myself a lifetime heretic. Even as a child, I was never very popular with my teachers, who labeled my questioning "disrespectful."

Although there were many years when I didn't much like God, I somehow trusted this all-knowing being enough to suspect that God wouldn't mind a little disrespect while I asked some hard questions about what I *truly* believed. And so in the midst of my cancer crisis at the age of thirty-seven, suspecting I didn't have much leisure time left to explore God, I stepped up the pace.

Staring death in the face, I made some spiritual decisions.

And the animals became the bellwether of my search. No longer can I support a vision of God or a religious belief that places humans at the top of a pyramid of value and special favor, with every other living thing positioned somewhere below. The only image I can hold is that of a table, and animals must have a seat at that table of life. In my heart I have never believed in a heaven reserved for humans only. And I have no interest in spending eternity in such a place!

My love for animals is so strong that I base my spiritual beliefs upon them. At the heart of this faith rests my belief in the undeniable voice of my own soul. Any religious doctrine that does not celebrate and hold sacred all of creation *feels* unacceptable to me. And I use the word *feel* literally. When I consider such belief systems, I feel sick to my stomach and hot with shame at our human arrogance.

Cancer taught me to trust my feelings and my intuition, and I am eternally grateful for that. Our culture places little or no value on inner knowing, but intuition is our homing system to our most honest selves, to our very core And my homing system tells me that humans and animals are truly on equal footing so far as the universe is concerned.

It is not my intention to have anyone denounce her or his religious affinity. Faith can be a healing grace of enormous proportion. But a little heresy, a little questioning, can lead to a clearer view of our own spirituality. Religious texts of any faith can be confusing. Interpreting what these doctrines actually say about animals, about humans, about souls, and about the heavens has kept sages and religious scholars busy arguing since the beginning of written human history. If even the most learned sages and theologians can't come to a consensus, perhaps each of us needs to decide for himself or herself what meaning we will ascribe to various spiritual teachings. For myself, I have decided that if there is a heaven, then animals are welcome there. The Bible that confused me as a child with its proclamation of humankind's dominion over the earth is the same text that reassures me: "Man hath no preeminence over the beast" (Ecclesiastes 3:19). And so I'll choose to believe Ecclesiastes over Genesis, because that is what my heart tells me to do. I encourage you to explore and trust your own interpretation of whatever religious text that you hold true.

For all the grace that animals bring to us, I believe we are obliged to somehow gift them in return. Animal communicator Sharon Callahan believes that we can care for the souls of animals as they have cared for ours:

> From years of communicating with animals telepathically and helping people understand their animals better, I have learned more than I ever imagined about the spiritual lives of animals. For those of us who have chosen a spiritual path, our animals' deepest wish is that we make the most of our commitment to that path. For in doing so, they are elevated, too. . . . We can repay our beloved animal companions for the bless-

ings of love they so freely offer us. We do this by simply nurturing our own spiritual lives and by treating our animals as the spiritual companions they are. Our animals have much to teach us about spirituality, but we must do our part so that they can do theirs.

Perhaps then, this could be *our* Blessing of the Animals: to explore and commit ourselves to our most actualized spiritual life, for both our honor and the honor of the animals. As we strive to live lives of authenticity, enchantment, and soulfulness, we will find ourselves off the lofty pyramid of dominion and into an embracing circle, exchanging with our animals blessing for blessing.

▼ ▼ ▼

Sex Link

In early summer after the banty chickens had raised several clutches of babies, our golden sex link laying hen, whom I call Sex Link, took to a straw-filled box of her own and began nesting. I was completely baffled by her behavior. Sex links are hybridized chickens designed for factory farms and are just about the most human-engineered animals imaginable. Virtually every instinct has been bred out of them. When my friend Jenny offered us Sex Link, I wasn't convinced that this overbred bird could handle life as a free-range chicken at Brightstar

Farm. But she laid beautiful brown eggs the size of beefsteak tomatoes, and that tilted the scales in her favor. It takes a lot of banty eggs to make a frittata.

Now Sex Link had stopped her incredible egg production, planted her enormous red-feathered butt in one of our hen-house nesting boxes, and cultivated that telltale look of re-signed determination that always comes over the face of a sitting hen. She took her sitting seriously, leaving her box only once daily for some water and a few bites of cracked corn.

Sex Link wasn't alone in her efforts. The banties had all raised one clutch each of spring chicks and were back on nests again. For banties, such behavior is the norm. No one told Sex Link that her kind simply didn't go broody, so she sat for weeks, long after I'd turned her four eggs into a quiche and long after most of the banty hens were parading tiny new chicks at their sides. Sadly, none of Sex Link's eggs had been fertile. Our rooster, Bogart, is a very small banty, and the simple maps of their bodies—Sex Link Texas and Bogart Rhode Island—was a blueprint for sterility. Bogart's lack of success with Sex Link was not from want of trying.

Perhaps because Sex Link was so big and exotic compared to the petite and agile banty hens, Bogie had claimed her as his favorite, spending many hours protectively ushering her around the yard. He'd approach Sex Link when he was "in the mood." With his ceremonial rooster dance and with his sparkling green wings, he'd do a routine that looked just like a matador trying to

entice a bull to the cape: fanning his wings, tippy-toeing in circles, thrusting his head forward and back. You could almost
hear the trumpets. All the banty hens fairly swooned at this display of unabashed masculinity and would drop low to the
ground in submission and anticipation. Not Sex Link. She
would look over his fluttering, fanning shoulders, spy some
enticing bug or bit of greenery, and step over Bogart to reach it.
During their actual attempts at a physical union, Bogie could
rarely stay balanced atop Sex Link's enormous shoulders long
enough to ensure the continuity of the species.

When I took Sex Link's eggs from her, I fully expected that
she would give up the quest and once again bestow those beautiful eggs of hers up on us, but it didn't happen. With her beak,
she continued to gently shift her imaginary eggs beneath her so
that they would all get "done" at the same time. I couldn't have
removed her from that nest with explosives. Impressed with her
incredible determination, I decided to offer her a chance at
motherhood. One morning I went to Burns Feed Store and
purchased three day-old sex link chicks. Carrying them out to
the henhouse, I uttered a prayer that Sex Link would find it
within her to step up to the next challenge of parenthood.

When hens hatch their own chicks, they begin a very soft
clucking sound to their eggs several days before hatching begins.
The chicks, still in the shell, begin peeping back. I didn't know
if this pre-birth communication was important to hen and

chick bonding, but there was nothing I could do about it anyway. The three chicks I carried in a small cardboard box had been born in an incubator and I had no idea if they would recognize a mother-cluck if they heard it—or if they would even recognize Sex Link as a fellow chicken.

I took the golden-colored chicks from the box and held them in my cupped hand. Sex Link looked up from her nest with her beady eyes and tilted her head my way. "Look," I said to her, "this is how it goes. First you sit on invisible eggs for three or four weeks. Then the Fairy Egg Mother comes along and . . . tadah!!" I thrust my hand with the peeping chicks into her nest, then stood back, held my breath, and waited. Sex Link's head and neck popped up instantly when she felt the movement beneath her. "Cluck?" she asked tentatively. "Cluck . . . cluck?" She shifted her bulk high off the nest, raised up onto her stout gray toes, and peered between her legs. Quickly she sat back down, her eyes round and incredulous. Her weight shifted to accommodate the action beneath her. She rose once more and looked at the commotion of fuzz under her legs. With infinite care, as though she were settling herself upon spun glass, she nestled down.

The sound began then, that sweet, clear mother-clucking that always tells me new life is on the way, new life has arrived. Her wings fluffed out into a protective umbrella and a tiny chick face poked out inquisitively from the thick bed of her breast feathers. Tenderly, lovingly, she pushed the chick back into the oven-warmth of her bosom. I returned to the house.

Now, a month later, I watch Sex Link slowly parade her brood through the herb beds and onto the lawn. When I approach her, her wings arc into an imposing fan and she curses me in gruff chicken expletives. I've seen her run dogs, cats, and crows out of the yard, and even Bogie keeps his distance these days. I used to wonder how it is that some women are able to open their hearts and homes to foster children, to any and all children, as though each child is her very own. Watching Sex Link tenderly guide her young among my peonies, I have no need to wonder anymore.

Phaedra

I was surprised to find myself so smitten with Phaedra. I've never been especially enchanted with llamas, probably because I had been spit upon by so many when I once worked for a baby zoo. When I first saw Phaedra, she was standing in a field of daisies, her fluffy white coat dusted with dried flowers and bits of grass. She looked like a tiny fairy, big-eyed, delicate, and graceful as a deer on her tapered white legs. She was much smaller than any of the other llamas in the field and I mistook her for a baby until her owner told me that something had gone awry in her growth centers and she was dwarfed. To me, her babyish look only added to her unique appeal. Something about her seemed almost magical. Phaedra had a serene and delicate gentleness about her I'd never seen in a llama, and my heart was instantly and hopelessly lost to her.

At the time, Lee and I were fantasizing that Brightstar could be a going business concern and we could possibly raise certain stock animals for profit. We had selected miniature donkeys for our business venture, not because they made phenomenally good business sense, but because we loved them and, frankly, I wanted a good excuse to have more of them around. As luck would have it, the donkeys would indeed make stable business partners. Profits from selling their babies, though nothing to break the bank, would go a long way toward keeping all the other animals on the farm fed and cared for. Meanwhile, our small core herd of five would provide us with wonderful fertilizer, yard-trimming services, and their incomparable old-soul donkey presence.

Llamas, however, were not in our business plan. Their market had gone "soft." So when Phaedra walked up to me and nuzzled my cheek with a nose as soft as feathers, I bit my lip and turned away toward the other pasture—the one that held the miniature donkeys. Although I left Phaedra standing in the field that day, my heart was with her constantly. I made excuses to go back to the farm where she lived just to see her again. As the months went by, I noticed that Phaedra was getting a bit thinner, and that her coat had less sheen to it than I had remembered, but I didn't think much about it. Our farm was busy with babies, and my concerns were for my animal family at home.

I didn't see Phaedra again for nearly a year, but late in the fall I managed to visit her. As she walked across the pasture to greet me, I could hardly believe that this was the same animal I'd seen the year before. Her coat was caked with mud and burrs and was a dull, lifeless gray. Blackflies swarmed at the thick yellow discharge around her eyes and feasted on her filthy ears until they drew blood. When I rested my hands on her back, rib and bone moved beneath my fingers. She was a skeleton.

Size and deformity had betrayed her. As the other llamas in the pasture had grown tall and powerful, Phaedra was no match for them at the hay and grain bins. Too small to compete for food, she waited and she starved. She became the object of the herd's abuse, as weakened animals often are, and was a special target of the herdsire, who would knock her off her feet to breed. The stud had struck her down endlessly, coming at her like a log battering ram, eventually breaking her small face and jaw. Afterward, Phaedra learned to stay on the ground most of the day, to avoid the attention of the stud. Then another complication set in. Phaedra's eyesight was failing, perhaps because of her injuries. She had no night vision and spotty vision at best during the day. A night-light burned in her barn, and she would sleep beneath it, unsteady on her feet if she left the circle of dim yellow light. All this was told to me by the young man who owned her. He was a kind and loving man, the situation with Phaedra being one of those tragic things that sometimes happens on a farm, with many, many animals all needing time, care, and attention. He had moved Phaedra away from the herd to her own small pasture, but still, she continued to fail.

From the moment I first saw Phaedra, I knew she belonged with me. Yet even in the midst of her terrible suffering, I didn't ask to bring her home. I tried to stay within the limits Lee and I had set for our farm. Our animal family was enormous. Our financial resources were limited. There was no money left for new animals. In tears, I told myself to be an adult while my heart cracked inside of me. I remembered the words I said to myself when I worked for a humane society and euthanized animals every day: "Susan, you can't save them all. You can't."

And so I returned home and Phaedra stayed in her pasture. Early next spring, I went to see her again. She had made it through winter, but she looked worse. Her owner told me that earlier that week, she had fallen and couldn't get to her feet without help. She was a filthy, bony bundle of health problems and vet bills, and I heard myself say, "Please let me take her home." The next thing I knew, she was in the back of my van, kneeling quietly on a cushion of straw as we drove home to Brightstar. I imagined that Lee would have fits when I got there. Of course he didn't.

Phaedra stumbled out of the van and into our pastures, a frail, unsteady creature with an uncertain future. She took a few hesitant steps toward our barn and stopped a moment to sniff the branch of an apple tree. Her lips pursed into a Betty Boop pucker, and she uttered a questioning sort of murmur and looked back at me. The heart performs miracles: I saw a dainty, glittering fairy blessing our pastures with beauty and tranquillity, where anyone else would have seen a ball of dirt on stick legs.

Phaedra became my summer project. Each day I sang songs to her about fairies while I washed the dirt and fly crusts off of her ears and eyes and worked the burrs out of her fur. I treated her sore, swollen eyes with drops and wiped bug repellent on her face and ears. One day I got industrious and cut off her matted hair with a pair of scissors. My hands blistered and my wrists ached for days, but the results were worth it. Beneath the old dead coat was a fine white blanket of soft fur. My hope was that love, good food, and good care would be enough to bring Phaedra back to health, but fate fought me at every turn. First, it was a bad abscess in her cheek, near her once-broken jaw. Then it was diarrhea brought on by the antibiotics to fight the abscess. Next she quit eating. Finally she developed an ulcer. I poured Maalox down her throat three times a day, marveling that she didn't spit it back at me. In time, I realized that Phaedra could no longer chew hay or grass, and that grain passed through her unchewed and undigested. I put her on a special pelleted formula. She turned her nose up at three different brands, then finally accepted the fourth. The vet became such a regular visitor that I joked with him about setting up a cot in our barn.

Weeks passed and I asked myself—as Lee often asked—what on earth was I doing. There were countless other projects, other tasks that needed my time and attention. Yet I let them fall by the wayside, focusing my energy on Phaedra, my precious, gentle fairy. For reasons I could never hope to explain to anyone, myself included, Phaedra simply enchanted me. I would find myself spending hours just watching her walk around the pasture or sprawl luxuriously in the sun. Sometimes she would gaze up at a flock of birds overhead or sniff at the bees on a cluster of clover. One day, in the soft breeze of a late summer afternoon, I saw her leap around the pasture like a gazelle, all four legs straight beneath her, springing high up into the air as she tossed her head left and right in rapturous abandon. It is my most precious memory of her.

Despite all my loving care, Phaedra failed to thrive. She lived in a state of frail health, not gaining much ground, occasionally losing some. Her vet and food bills were hitting the catastrophic mark when I told Lee, out of shame for my lack of more mature and logical behavior, that I wouldn't spend any more money on her, that I would put her to sleep before she ran up any more big bills. Lee saw the pain in my eyes and, trying to spare me and our shrinking wallet, said, "No more charity cases, okay?" I turned away and muttered, "Yes, okay."

For the next few days, those words echoed in my head: *no*

more charity cases. I've learned to listen carefully when my inner buzzer goes off, as it was doing, because it usually means that I'm about to learn something of importance, if I listen closely and keep my mind and heart wide open.

One evening later that week, I sat in the barn with Phaedra and watched as she ate one or two pellets at a time. I asked her out loud the questions I had only asked myself. I asked her what she was doing at our farm, why she had called so strongly to me, and what she needed to teach me. Sitting on a bucket beside her, I closed my eyes and reached out my arms to her, waiting for whatever thoughts might come to me.

No more charity cases. Visions of a lifetime of hurt and lost animals drifted up before me. I had taken them all home—dogs, kittens, birds, half-squashed toads—and spent my last dime on them. I loved them, found them new homes, sometimes healed them, too often buried them. I remembered telling Lee before we were married that sometimes my affinity for animals wouldn't seem so cute. It would involve stopping in the middle of the road to carry a snake to a curb when we were already late for a party. Or it might involve a bathtub full of some sick creature that honks or cries all night. It would be money and emotion and tears spent on some broken, lost sick being. "You will get sick of it, and sick of me," I told him. He had not, or if so, only fleetingly. *I* was getting sick of it, sorry for it, ashamed of it. *Ashamed of it.* It's only an animal. Are all llamas that ugly? Why don't you put your energy into *people* charities? It seemed I had spent a lifetime explaining, justifying, apologizing. Even with a book about the virtues of animals to my credit, I still felt shame.

Could I have chosen my passion, I would not have chosen animals. In my desperate need to be liked, I would have selected a more politically correct cause on which to spend my life's passion. But I did not *choose*, I *was chosen*. Chosen long before I could even talk. My first words were about animals; my first joys, my first death, and my first births involved animals. When I was stricken with cancer in my late thirties, it was a lifetime of experience with animals living and dying in my home and in my arms that offered me a vision of healing. In a very real sense, animals had given me my life.

I heard Phaedra finish the last of her pellets. In the outstretched circle of my arms, she settled down on her knees and began working her cud. I stayed very still and continued to listen. Phaedra, for all the effort of her care, had brought me so many good things. In the hours I had spent with her, she had brought me back to a sense of childlike mystery. With Phaedra in the pasture, I could believe in fairies again. I could stop and take time to sit and daydream. Her gentle nature calmed me and brought me many moments of quiet and thanksgiving. She shared with me her joy and steadfast companionship. For what I had given her, she had given me back tenfold. *Tenfold.* This is how I tithe. My eyes flew open and met the quiet brown sea of Phaedra's kindly gaze. Her face was soft, her eyes clear and bottomless. The banana ears she swiveled toward me were white and clean. She leaned into me and gently sniffed my face. When I rubbed her neck, I realized that her bones were beginning to disappear behind a new layer of muscle. There had been improvements, albeit small ones. She would be fine. We would be fine. Shame melted for the time being. I knew it would return, but each time I would feel the sting of it less and less. This is how I tithe, not with money or checks but with time and love willingly given to a decades-long chain of animals who found their way to me, who chose me, healed me, empowered me: the charity cases. God grant me a never-ending stream of charity cases. When I left the barn that night and returned to the house, it was to tell Lee that I would be cutting off my very arms and legs if there were no place at our farm for charity cases. And of course he understood. It was I who needed to understand, and it was Phaedra who had chosen to teach me.

Behind the Door
by Penelope Ann Thoms

As the only chaplain on duty at a Catholic hospital in Sonoma County, I was frequently called to solve the theological/

medical concerns of patients and their doctors. One evening I was paged into the Cardiac Care Unit, where a middle-aged man was to undergo bypass surgery. The doctor explained to me that this gentleman had been flown in from Southern California because of massive heart failure and the procedure would effectively save his life. However, the doctor couldn't proceed with the operation because the patient refused to sign the consent forms, saying he didn't deserve the operation. Would I talk to him?

"John" was in his mid-sixties. After I introduced myself as the hospital chaplain his response was immediate: "No God talk, Chaplain, I left the church a long time ago." Of course, what John didn't know was that this is a challenge to any chaplain, and I became determined to discover what his ecclesial divorce was all about.

John had been an active member of a large mainstream denomination for all of his life. He and his family had attended and supported, physically and financially, one church, in the same town where he grew up. One evening during an adult education program on "visualizing God in your life," John was asked to imagine a door behind which was an image of God. After concentrating on this image, participants were asked to open the door and describe what they saw.

At this point in his story, John's eyes grew moist and he turned his face away from me. "I'm too embarrassed to tell you what was behind my door." Imagining all sorts of demonic possibilities, I was readying the appropriate "pastoral response." "What did you see, John, when you opened the door?"

Trembling, John turned his sad eyes toward mine. "I saw a dog."

"A dog?"

"Well, not just any dog. My dog. My dog Molly, who had just died. The instructor didn't think that was the right answer and I guess it wasn't; but that was what I saw and I told him so. He suggested I go home and think about how I saw God. I was so embarrassed that I never went back."

"Tell me about Molly."

"She was a golden retriever. I found her at the pound and she was the best dog our family could have had. She protected the children when they were little—always worrying about them. I traveled a great deal and she was great company for my wife, who never felt alone when Molly was in the house. She loved me unconditionally, although I wasn't always the best father or husband; no matter what I looked like or how my day had been, Molly always greeted me like I was a king."

"Let me see. Molly protected your children from harm, comforted your wife in her loneliness, and loved you unconditionally. Sounds like Molly and God had a lot in common. In fact, it sounds like Molly is still with you in your memory, as God is with you now. And I bet Molly would want you to have your operation, to go home to your family."

John had his operation. I didn't once mention that "God" is

"dog" spelled backwards, or that I raised golden retrievers (what if Molly had been a cat!) and that I often saw the love of God in the eyes of Spec, Buck, Moose, Clare, or Max. But I think I could have said those things because God has a sense of humor. I'm sure God put me in the room with John for just that reason.

CHAPTER THREE

A Language of the Heart: Communicating with Animals

"If you talk with the animals they will talk with you and you will know each other. If you do not talk to them, you will not know them, and what you do not know, you will fear. What one fears one destroys."

— CHIEF DAN GEORGE

My friend Claire lived in a rental house with a lease agreement that included care of the previous owner's eleven-year-old malamute mix, Shekhinah. During those first few weeks, Claire and Shekhinah were going through that getting-to-know-you stage, when Claire called me and said, "Shekhinah looks at me as though she's trying to tell me something. I feel so guilty because I have no idea what's going on inside her head. And I say to her 'Darn, if only Susan were here, she'd know what you are trying to say!'"

I had to disappoint her. I do not read dogs' minds. My own mind is a mystery to me most of the time. Animal communication is a recurring theme people discuss with me at workshops and conferences. Too often, the discussion goes something like this: "My German shepherd nearly died last week. I'd been communicating with her and I was sure her problem was *this*, but it was really *that*, and I feel awful that I didn't hear her correctly." Or "My Angora rabbit got infested with maggots and I had no idea until it was too late. I'll never forgive myself. If I'd loved her enough, I know I'd have sensed what was going on with her. Surely, she was trying to tell me and I just wasn't listening." Or "I took these classes and got lots of videos and tapes on interspecies communication and I still can't do it. There must be something wrong with me."

There are people who can communicate telepathically with animals. I no longer doubt that this phenomenon exists. There are too many amazing, verifiable stories of direct and accurate communication between animals and skilled communicators, also called animal psychics. From time to time, I have had communications like these with my animals, and hundreds of people have written me detailing astonishing and frequently unexpected "conversations" with their own animals. Often, these communications just happened, leaving the owners stunned and delighted—and a little hesitant about sharing their experiences. "My husband will think I'm going nuts," one says, or "I can hardly believe this myself. How can I expect anyone else to?" Frankly, I think it would be unusual to go through a lifetime with an animal and *not* have miracle moments when you simply knew what your animal was telling you. However, difficulties can arise when we try to communicate with our animal companions on our schedule and according to our needs, and find that we cannot manage to repeat our conversational successes at will. I am one of these people—the telepathically challenged!

Many readers assume I am an animal psychic, and they are terribly disappointed to find out that I am not. I too am disappointed that I am not. I even took a class designed to teach telepathic or intuitive communication with animals. The flyer said that in two days we would have the basics down for mental communication with our animal partners. Some of the participants at that workshop did indeed go home with a new understanding and the ability to "talk" with their animals. I believe that everyone is capable, to differing degrees, of honing mental abilities like these. These intuitive abilities have always been part of our natural repertoire of communication. But I have also come to believe that developing effective and *consistent* telepathic communication with animals takes a tremendous amount of effort and commitment for most people. Some of the participants at the workshop I attended had been practicing this skill for years, and fretted that their abilities are still very much hit or miss. One of the best animal communicators I know, Sharon Callahan, said that although she is regularly asked to teach animal communication workshops, she has no interest in doing so. "What I'd really have to teach is deep meditation. You can't 'hear' what's in an animal's mind until you empty the noise out of your own, and that can take months or years of meditation practice—at least it has for me. Most people don't have the time or the commitment for this sort of work. It takes total focus, and total dedication. You have to want it that much."

Whenever I am feeling remorse about all that I don't know about my animal companions' inner needs, I recall Callahan's words. Total dedication to sharpening my skills in telepathic communication—animal or otherwise—is not a priority in my life. I know that my strongest skills lie in writing and speaking on behalf of animals. Animal communicators like Callahan are there to help me talk to my animals when the need arises and my own communication skills are not enough. Communicating with animals telepathically is an exciting area of the human/animal relationship that is becoming more accepted by many animal lovers. However, communication of this kind is serious lifework that skilled people develop over years. On those days when Arrow looks up at me and gazes intensely into my eyes—and I feel like a sorry excuse for a partner because I have no idea whether she is telling me she is hungry, she loves me, or she thinks there's life on Pluto—I am forced to remind myself that I can't be good at everything.

Most of the time I feel I understand my animal family and

can intuit their needs quite well. Yet I have also had animals sicken and die in my home because I was distracted and missed what were obvious signals of terrible distress. Good communication with my animals, telepathic or other, isn't a given for me. Sometimes it's there, sometimes it's not. Frequently during the past year, I have been away from home because of my work. Arrow has developed skin problems during this time and has even taken to pooping in my office when I am gone. I do not know if she fears that I am not coming back, or if she misses me too much when I am away, or if her problems are simply allergies and indigestion. We don't understand each other very well sometimes, and it's frustrating and upsetting when I come home from a long trip to find her sulky and depressed, her lush brown coat mottled with scabs. So I understand what people feel when they tell me of their shame and guilt over the missed communications between themselves and their animal partners.

Yet at times luck, grace, and the cosmos align and I have a moment with an animal when the communication feels clear and true. Recently I had an experience like that with Arrow. In addition to her skin problems and bad toilet habits, Arrow regularly escapes from our yard when I am out of town. When I am home, our fences and hedging do a fair job of convincing Arrow to stay in the backyard and pastures, but when I leave for more than a day or two, no fencing on earth will hold her.

Invariably Lee or our house sitter will find her sitting on the front porch, waiting, when they return home. Our house is close to a country road that doesn't have a lot of traffic, but the few cars that go by seem to fly. The notion of Arrow heading out onto that road terrifies me. Not long ago, I was attending a conference on animals and spirituality where I participated in a guided meditation on communicating with animals, and Arrow came instantly to mind. I saw her barking loudly and excitedly. Then the word *sentinel* formed in my mind. When I returned home later that week, I learned that Arrow had of course left the yard several times and enthroned herself on the front porch.

Being away from home a lot is not easy for me, and worrying about the safety of my beloved dog makes it all the harder. Instead of directing my distress at Arrow, I worked to quiet my thoughts as suggested at the conference to understand what was driving Arrow to her potentially deadly escapes. I brought Arrow's face to mind and thought, *Why the front porch?* An answer came instantly—more quickly than my own mind usually formulates ideas: *Because you never come in the back door. You return to the front door first.* Then the word *sentinel* came to mind again. And I understood: Arrow, my self-appointed guardian and sentinel, was standing watch for me. I just *knew* it. I still do not know how to keep Arrow in the yard, but at least I feel as though I understand the situation better. What's more, I can actually appreciate what she is trying to do. Arrow has a sense of mission about these escapes and they deserve my acknowledgment. Clearly, she takes her work as sentinel seriously, and any good work deserves recognition and appreciation.

Many people have shared far more dramatic telepathic animal moments with me. Robin Moore told me about an unusual event that took place many years ago when she was still in college. She was home for the weekend when she was awakened abruptly one morning by a piercing scream: "Daddy, help me!" She said it seemed as though the message had been shouted directly into her ear. She lay in bed for a moment, heart racing, still half asleep, trying to understand what she'd just heard. All was still in the house and yard. Then she heard a slight muffled sound coming from outside. Looking out her window, she saw what looked like a small patch of snow on the grass. Beside it was a cat, who pawed at the white object and pushed it around on the lawn. It took only a few seconds for her to realize that the "snow" was a small, injured white dove. Robin's parents had a pair of white doves. Evidently, the birds had nested once and hatched one egg, a female. Later that year, the mother bird had escaped, leaving father and daughter in the outside aviary.

Robin took the mortally wounded dove from the cat and ran into the house, waking her parents, calling, "The mother dove came back! She's terribly hurt!" Robin's mother took one look at the injured bird and said, "That's not the mother. It's the daughter."

Goose bumps rose on Robin's skin: "I realized who had screamed, 'Daddy, help me!' I do not consider myself psychic. But even my scientific nature has to accept the fact that I received and translated the distress cry of another species." Robin and her parents put the dying bird back into the aviary, the only home the dove had ever known. They speculated that somehow the family cat had managed to pull the dove through the wire mesh.

Because I cannot claim great talents as a telepathic communicator, I have devised other, more practical ways of being in communication with my animal companions. First and foremost, I talk to my animals all the time. And I imagine that on some level they understand exactly what I am saying. The simple act of speaking respectfully to them seems to place me within their circle of partnership and equality. I speak to bugs, chickens, birds, trees, and all the other beings here on our farm. When I am preparing for a trip, I tell the animals when and where I am going and that I will be returning. I ask Sisi, the matriarch donkey, to take care of the barn and its residents. I tell Pumpkin to take care of Lee. The chickens and Mirella, our huntress cat, get warned to keep on the alert for coyotes. Arrow is asked to guard the chickens and the cats. Sometimes I am able to take Arrow along with me, and I tell her to "get ready."

In his inspiring book *Talking with Nature*, Australian rancher Michael Roads writes about his astounding success at "asking" wallabies to please not eat his pasture grass. "I fairly yelled my message to all the wallabies that might listen," he writes. "It sounded something like this: 'I don't know if you wallabies can hear me, but I am offering an agreement with you by which we each meet our own needs. I am asking that you stop eating our pasture, and in exchange for this I will see to it that nobody shoots you again. However, because I realize that I must share this land with you, I will allow you to graze around the outside of the paddock. Please don't take more than twenty yards.' " Within weeks, the pasture was so thick, he was able to add a dozen more stock animals to his farm. Others have told me of similar successes in asking deer to stay out of gardens or coyotes to spare their chickens.

At Brightstar Farm, I speak out loud to the legion of moles in our area and ask them to stay off our lawns. As a fair trade, I invite them to do their earthwork in the flower beds, driveway, and pasture areas. We have had few mole mounds on our lawns since. But during one of my trips away, Lee called me and asked if we had a mole trap. "Why?" I asked. "Because there must be twenty huge mole mounds on the lawn this morning. I don't know where they all came from, but they came by the truckload a couple days after you left." As soon as I got home, I sat on our front porch and begged the moles to please leave the lawns alone. I put the mole trap on the porch as a reminder, and warned the moles that if they got near our buried phone cables, I would have to start getting violent with them. Within a couple of days—I am not kidding—they were completely gone. It was almost eerie. Lee started calling me Lord of the Moles.

I had similar conversations with the black wasps and the yellow jackets who nested on our deck this past summer. So far we have all lived together without incident, but I have told them I am prepared to move them out if they go on the offensive. Anyone who insists on scientific proof that these insects or any of the animals hear me will not get an argument from me. I cannot prove that my conversations serve the good of any creature but me. Yet I am not prepared to dismiss the possibility, either. I think about the scientists who send radio messages out to the galaxies, searching for some return signal from the stars that will assure humankind that we are not alone in the universe. These scientists are doing what I am doing when I speak to my donkeys. All of us are giving intrinsic approval to rich possibilities of communication with life other than our own kind. If we did not believe in interspecies/interstellar communication, we wouldn't be wasting our words or our airwaves.

If I were to receive incontrovertible proof that the conversations between my animals and me are just a one-way communiqué, that would be just fine, too. The process of speaking in a respectful manner to creation helps me feel connected to the earth and its many living relatives. Also, it is impossible to talk to worms and chickens without putting a firm lid on my inbred human arrogance—and that is a good thing.

At the suggestion of a horse trainer, who said that she always has better luck training her horses if she can mentally picture for them the maneuver she wants them to perform, I try to talk to my animals with mental pictures as well as words. So when I am planning to trim the donkeys' hooves, I tell them so. I also picture the process in my mind and imagine the box of trimming tools in my hands and their standing quietly and contentedly as I work.

A remarkable woman, Temple Grandin, wrote a fascinating book, *Thinking in Pictures and Other Reports from My Life with Autism.* Grandin has been able to overcome many of the limitations of her autism and is now an international lecturer, not only about autism, but about her work as an animal scientist and developer of humane livestock-handling equipment. Grandin has designed one-third of all the livestock-handling equipment used in the United States, including a humane procedure for kosher slaughter. When asked about her unparalleled ability to create such cattle-respectful equipment, Grandin claims that she thinks not in words, but in pictures, and theorizes that cows—and other animals—do the same. She literally puts herself into the cows' place of confinement and sees the world through their eyes. Empathetic and compassionate, Temple shares a special bond with cattle, whom she believes share her uncommon "sight." Her book inspired me to practice thinking in pictures when I try to communicate with my animals.

Sometimes, in trying to decipher the motives of their animal companions, people discount the most obvious tool animals have of communicating with us: body language. Each animal species has its own unique postures and forms of bodily expression. From the startled jerk of a horse's head to the intent flicking of a cat's tail, animals—including humans—are a complex symphony of physical communication. Dogs will pant not just from heat but from nervousness or pain. Cats lick themselves not only for cleanliness but when they are embarrassed or confused. Mirella, our acrobat cat, will go into a furious washing spell when she misses a jump to a tree limb or lands clumsily on a flight to the top of the refrigerator. My donkeys don't have the highly developed instinct to flee that horses do when startled. Instead, they plant themselves into the ground like boulders and stand with ears alert as radar dishes. When I see them in that position, I know something strange is in the yard. It could be a person, an animal, or a wind-blown plastic milk jug. Pumpkin puffs up her huge orange head crest and shouts, "Hello! *Hello!*" when she's happy. Guests who don't know her well often think she's angry or about to bite when she "flares up."

How easy it is to misread an animal's body language when there are so many languages to learn! Yet some people speak this most ancient of languages eloquently. I have seen this kind of communication most often between horses and riders. To ride well, to even stay seated, one almost needs to become part of the horse, and this requires an intention and focus that seems to transcend training and commands. Johanna, a young neighbor of ours, and her beloved pony, Barney, can speak to each other body to body. I have seen it in the way she sits atop him as he canters across their sheep pasture, their bodies melded from her supple waist down to his burnished hooves. The standard training is all there, but Johanna and Barney speak to each other, muscle to muscle. Perhaps part of our age-old fascination with horses has to do with this special method of communication we share with them.

I have also come to trust in a special kind of communication with animals that goes far beyond words. I feel this bond most often in the simplest interaction with animals: When I am holding Flora on my lap and she is batting gently at my hand, when I go outside to feed the donkeys and see them holding me with their eyes from across the barnyard. Sometimes Pumpkin will catch my eye from her perch and gaze at my face and I will feel the intimacy between us fill the quiet room. These communications are food for my soul. They wash over me with a flood of peace, reminding me of my place at the table of my life. In these moments, I feel most at home in this world. I call this exquisite form of communication "communion." In communion, I am making no effort to speak to my animals. Instead, I am reveling in moments of just *being* with them.

We who treasure our communication with animals, in whatever form it takes, must also be willing to explore the shadow side of this special bond with animals. In what ways may we be harming the animals we cherish with our beliefs about communication? For many years, I have been a champion of anthropomorphism, which is the tendency to assign human attributes and characteristics to animals. Believing that we can somehow interpret what our animals may be thinking or trying to tell us is a kind of anthropomorphism. Long maligned as a disease and a delusion (according to behaviorist John S. Kennedy), anthropomorphism has been regarded by science as a contaminator of objective research. "Young scientists have to be specifically trained to resist the temptation to interpret the behavior of other species in terms of their normal behavior-recognition mechanisms," warns animal behaviorist David McFarland. The problem with this extreme negative response to anthropomorphism is that young scientists may never consider that animals may also feel joy, love, curiosity, concern, mercy, or any one of a thousand other attributes humankind has claimed for itself alone.

Fortunately, I have never been subject to the rigid constraints of science where animals are concerned. And I have always wondered what was so wrong with assuming that my dog or cat felt sad, got bored, or loved me—just as I got bored, felt sad, and loved my animals. As philosopher Mary Midgely explains it, "Animals are not just one of the things with which people amuse themselves, like chewing gum and water skis, *they are the group to which people belong.* We are not just rather like animals. We *are* animals."

What, really, is the problem with anthropomorphism? In *When Elephants Weep: The Emotional Lives of Animals,* author Jeffrey Moussaieff Masson discusses the double-edged sword of anthropomorphism. He begins his book with a great story that hints at what can happen when we view animals through the tiny lens of our human projections:

> In 1987 I visited a south Indian game reserve known for its wild elephants. Early one morning I set out with a friend to walk in the forest. After a mile or so, we came across a herd of about ten elephants, including small calves, peacefully grazing. My friend stopped at a respectful distance, but I walked closer.... One large elephant looked toward me and flapped his ears.
>
> Knowing nothing about elephants, I had no idea that this was a warning. Blissfully ignorant, as if I were in a zoo or in the presence of Babar or some other storybook elephant, I felt it was time to commune with the elephants. Remembering a Sanskrit verse for saluting Ganesha, the Hindu God who takes elephant form, I called *"Bhoh, gajendra"*—Greetings, Lord of the Elephants.

The elephant trumpeted; for a second I thought it was his return greeting. Then his sudden, surprisingly agile turn and thundering charge in my direction made it all too clear that he did not participate in my elephant fantasies. I was aghast to see a two-ton animal come hurtling toward me. It was not cute and did not resemble Ganesha. I turned and ran wildly.... He clearly meant to see me dead, to knock me down with his trunk and trample me.... I remember thinking, "How could you have been so stupid as to approach a wild elephant?"

Masson stumbles in the tall grass and falls, and the charging elephant luckily loses sight of him and eventually moves back to the herd. "Rudimentary knowledge of elephants would have kept me safe," Masson continues. "A herd with small calves is particularly alert to danger; elephants don't like their space invaded; flapping ears are a direct warning. The encounter itself was nothing but a projection of my own wish that a wild elephant would want to meet me. I was wrong to think that I could communicate with a strange elephant under these circumstances. Yet he communicated very clearly to me: he was angry and I should leave."

Masson's example speaks to the heart of the anthropomorphism conflict: There is nothing wrong with believing that animals feel complex emotions and lead rich emotional lives, as we do. It seems obvious to everyone but the scientific community that animals do so, and certainly it seems most obvious to those of us who have shared our lives and homes with animals. We do not need proof. We can trust our collective gut on this one. But we do a supreme disservice to animals when we assume that they feel what we feel, in the way we feel it.

We do not know what a cow feels as her calf is led away and sold. When we hear her harsh bellows of distress, we only imagine that she may be saying, "Please, no." We can only project what we might feel in similar circumstances. This projection is a legitimate starting place, but it is *not* the end of the path. We are human animals. We are not cows. To thrust our fantasies upon them is to discredit their uniqueness and to disregard the mystery of their expression. It does not allow for the possibility that a cow may suffer in ways that we, as humans, cannot even imagine. We may see our animal companions grieving over a lost companion or the loss of a familiar home and know in our very bones that what we are seeing is grief, yet we can never know what grief feels like in that animal's body and soul.

When mother animals destroy or abandon their young, we may say to ourselves, "That cat was a despicable mother . . . That dog was so uncaring she left her young to die . . . The rabbit murdered her babies!" And yet we cannot truly know an animal's motivation. Perhaps the babies were ill in some way we could never see. Maybe the mother animal was terrified that her babies had been "discovered" by strangers and were no longer safe, and she killed them to protect them from an imagined greater harm. Maybe something in her own body told her she would not have enough food or strength to provide for her offspring. We can never know the inner life of an animal with any degree of certainty, any more than we can truly know the inner life of a fellow human being. And that is why anthropomorphism can be dangerous, and why our best attempts at communicating with animals must be tempered with awe and respect for all that we do not know and will never know. By gifting animals with human characteristics, values, or virtues, we may be diminishing an inner brilliance animals possess that lies far beyond our everyday imaginings. We must let animals be animals. While it is important to emphasize our similarities with animals, we must also grant them their differences, their uniqueness, their mysteries.

Those of us who pride ourselves on our dedication to the welfare of the animals in our homes are often embarrassed when we find that our love is not enough to pave a veritable freeway of communication between us. Yet we do not have perfect communication with our children, our spouses, our friends, and colleagues at work. Why should we expect to communicate perfectly with our animals? Real communication with animals is not about our own agenda or what we want our animals to "tell" us. It is about listening and being patient, and about the power of good intentions. If we are attentive, we *will* get a sense of what the animals are saying.

▼ ▼ ▼

Evinrude

Whenever Lee introduces guests to our tabby cat, Evinrude, he always says, "This is Evinrude, the fish." I was shopping for goldfish at a local pet store when I got sidetracked by an eight-week-old, brick-nosed gray tabby. I had always wanted a plain gray tabby cat. The cats that found me seemed to be every color under the sun, but none of them were gray tabbies. And so Evinrude came home with me. When Lee came home from work that evening and spied Evinrude peering solemnly out at him from under our bed, he said, "Is that the fish you were shopping for this afternoon?"

I said, "Yes."

Evinrude settled in comfortably to his new home and quickly adopted Bear, our huge orange tom, as his most beloved friend. All it took was one tentative nose-to-nose sniff. Bear rubbed against the tiny kitten's face and Evinrude returned the gesture with a kiss. The attraction was instant and mutual and we rarely saw the two cats apart for the next year. They would sleep together in a colorful jumble of loose legs and tails. They shared the same food bowl, the same end of the litter box, the same lazy spot of sun on the floor in the afternoon. Each evening the devoted buddies settled down together to gently wash each other's ears and feet, and purr a bass duet of absolute contentment. I never saw two cats enjoy each other's company more.

When I made the heartbreaking decision to have Bear euthanized after his endless and agonizing series of bladder and kidney infections, I knew that the death of this wise red king would be unspeakably painful for both Evinrude and me. Under the weight of my own grief, I watched Evinrude prowl through the house like smoke blowing fitfully through empty rooms. My grief was silent, but Evinrude gave intense, physical expression to his. At first he paced the halls and rooms looking for Bear. He cried to me often and long, and stared out of windows for endless hours. Some evenings he would run up and down the hall, looking, looking, looking, flicking his long whiskers. After a few weeks, he became listless and distracted, missing days at the food bowl. I never saw him lounging in the now-forgotten spot in the sun.

Finally, in an apparent effort to replace the cuddling affection he had shared with Bear, Evinrude began making earnest overtures of friendship to Arrow. His determined efforts at washing her face and ears seemed to confuse Arrow at first. She would back away from him and whine, ears down and tail tucked, not so much in submissiveness, I thought, but in a kind of startled perplexity. But Evinrude had Arrow pegged well. Arrow inhales affection and delights in new friends. Before long, Arrow began to accept all the new and unusual attention from the determined tabby, and they became pals. Although Arrow still won't let Evinrude sleep with her, she seems to thoroughly enjoy his hearty head-rubs against her cheek, and will stand patiently as he roams under her legs, wrapping his rope of a tail over her flanks. Many times each day, I will look out to the back porch and see Arrow and Evinrude sitting side by side, enjoying moments of a subtle, wordless companionship.

With Arrow standing in as an adequate Bear substitute, I thought that Evinrude's grieving was behind him. But a few months after Bear's death, I noticed some unusual changes in Evinrude's behavior. He began to take on many of Bear's old mannerisms. In the mornings, just as Bear had done, Evinrude began escorting me to the barn when I did the daily chores. When I sat down to breakfast, Evinrude would suddenly throw himself across my feet, nibble my ankles, and bat at my shoelaces. Bear, too, had been transfixed with feet and shoes from his earliest kitten days, and would embrace any shoe that stayed in one place long enough for him to claim and cuddle it. One night Evinrude took over Bear's sleeping place on my bed and became a regular fixture on my pillow after that. He took to napping on his back with his feet in the air, just like Bear.

These new routines were all fine with me, with the exception of one: Evinrude began to yowl. He would follow me from room to room and warble in my face nonstop. This sound wasn't anything like a conversational meow. It was a caterwaul, a bellow, a screeching wail. Bear had howled that way too, because of his bladder pain. But I couldn't figure out why Evinrude howled, other than to make the walls rattle. The sound was intolerable. Unable to stand it any longer, I sat down in front of

Evinrude's big, bellowing face one day and howled back at him, asking, "What are you *doing*? Why do you want to drive me crazy?" He quickly sat down in front of me. His mouth snapped shut and he stared at my furrowed brow with eyes like cool yellow moons. Little that comes to me intuitively comes in words. More often, it is a rush of feelings, a stream of thoughts, or a riot of colorful mental pictures. This time, as soon as Evinrude looked into my eyes, I had a vivid memory of Bear's last night with me.

Bear was huge, and the euthanol injection given him by our vet took a long time to take effect. I had been holding Bear in a blanket on my lap for nearly an hour, waiting for him to expire. But he laid there fast asleep, snoring heavily, curled on my knees like a carrot-colored lap robe. The vet assured me she had given Bear enough solution and it was only a matter of time. My tears turned Bear and me into wet messes as I waited. I was so focused on Bear that I hadn't noticed Evinrude lying at my feet watching the whole sad process. Suddenly he leaped into my lap. Then he walked over my legs to Bear and began gently sniffing Bear's face with intense curiosity. He sniffed everywhere with his brick-red nose and long, twig-like whiskers—Bear's ears, closed eyes, paws, nose, tail—moving his head slowly up and down the full length of his dying friend. In a state of deep concentration, Evinrude paused a moment, then leaned forward with eyes squeezed shut and began intently kneading Bear's chest with his thick paws. His feet moving rhythmically in quick dancelike steps, Evinrude pressed the air out of Bear's lungs. Bear made no effort to inhale. As the air flowed out and up, Bear's spirit followed and he was gone, instantly and at last.

Now, as Evinrude and I looked at each other, our faces mere inches apart, the memory of that moment hung in the air between us. As I recalled that night so clearly, I knew then what the yowling was all about. Evinrude had taken up Bear's habits, good and bad, yowling and all, because something else had transpired there in my lap the night that Bear died. Something I didn't see. Somehow I understood that the two friends had made a pact in those brief moments on my lap. Evinrude had agreed to take care of me. Bear had always been my self-appointed guardian and chaperone, and he was not willing to release his job easily. That was why death had come so slowly. In taking over Bear's job, Evinrude had assumed Bear's habits as well. The yowling was not meant to bother me, but to remind me that I was still watched over and protected in the spirit of Bear.

How I knew this I cannot say, but the truth of it resonated within me swiftly and completely. I picked up Evinrude and held him in my arms and thanked him for all his good work on my behalf. He had been true to his "word" to Bear, and I told him how proud I was of him. After that, not surprisingly, his yowling decreased dramatically.

A few years ago, I lost a good friend to cancer. Her husband sent me a raincoat she used to wear and her leather briefcase.

When I wear the coat and carry the leather case, I feel a bit of Debbie wrapped around me, comforting me. I wonder, watching Evinrude lying belly up, feet to the sky, if somehow he keeps a little bit of Bear close by in wearing those old habits of his beloved friend.

Barbara's Story
by Sharon Callahan

In 1974, Barbara, a female Asian elephant, was captured by Asian elephant trainers, known as mahouts. Barbara was singled out because of her age, beauty, and disposition. The mahouts, riding on trained elephants, walked into the herd and dropped ropes around Barbara's neck and legs, dragging her from her family and jungle home and changing her life forever. Taken to a logging camp, she was then tied to a tree while she learned to tolerate life in "civilization." Very loving and intelligent, Barbara learned what was expected of her in just a few weeks. She was then loaded into a wooden crate and sent to America, having been purchased along with seven other elephants by a circus.

For several months Barbara and her new family were taught a variety of tricks such as standing on their hind legs, holding each other's tails, and lying on their sides. Due to their great intelligence Barbara and the other elephants did not find the tricks difficult, but the work was unnatural and very stressful.

For the next twelve years, Barbara and her new elephant family performed in circuses traveling throughout the United States.

At fourteen years of age Barbara was retired to a breeding farm along with others from her elephant family. During this time Barbara began to lose weight. Many tests were performed, but all came up negative and no answer could be found for her loss of weight. Several baby elephants were born during this time, but Barbara was unable to conceive. She lost weight throughout the next twelve years, ultimately losing a total of 2,000 pounds. Because she was so emaciated Barbara was finally separated from her family and put in solitary confinement, where she entered a deep depression.

Due largely to the efforts of Carol Buckley, founder and director of the Elephant Sanctuary in Hohenwald, Tennessee (see the Resources section), Barbara was finally relocated and became a resident of the nation's only natural habitat refuge for Asian elephants.

In February of 1997, Carol contacted me about Barbara's condition. Despite all the love and affection showered on her by Carol, wholesome food, expert veterinary care, and the freedom of the sanctuary grounds, Barbara remained frail. She seemed to carry the weight of the world on her shoulders. The inch-deep scar around her neck, a testament to her struggle as she was dragged from her original elephant family, was very sensitive to the touch. Barbara didn't trumpet the way elephants usually do, and as far as anyone knew, she never had. Carol thought perhaps her larynx had been damaged as she was dragged from her family by the mahouts—or perhaps she had been silenced by grief. Carol was very concerned.

When I communicated with Barbara for the first time and asked her what she was experiencing, I was overcome by feelings of profound sadness and a deep sense of loss unlike anything I had ever felt before. Nothing in my life experience, and I have experienced several tragic losses, came even close to what Barbara was feeling. Barbara wanted Carol to know that she was deeply appreciative of her new home and the wonderful care she was receiving, but that she was the bearer of the grief of her species and that she could not begin to heal herself until she was able to give voice to the urgent message of her brothers and sisters.

As of this writing, I have worked with Barbara as an animal communicator for sixteen months. In this time Barbara revealed to me not only the details of her own personal suffering, but the profound purpose of the elephants and the suffering they all experience when that purpose is thwarted. Jenny and Tara, the Sanctuary's other resident elephants, have contributed much to my understanding as well.

Below is a composite of communications I've received from Barbara over the months:

> I speak now as a single manifestation of the great ones
> you call Elephant. I have been sent as an emissary

during this enormous time of planetary transformation to speak for those of my kind who have no voice,
and for those who have gone on into the realms of
White Love. When we are together nothing can separate us but the ropes and guns and greed of humankind. We care deeply for each other, and we move and
breathe as one great gray and luminous heart. I have
seen one lost calf turn a whole herd wild with grief and
rage. What one feels, so do we all feel, and as much as
we are attuned to one another, we are attuned to the
Great Mother Earth herself: her pain, the scars upon
her body, the tears of her great rivers as they attempt
to remove impurities from her quivering form, the
clouds of brown particles that surround her glittering
countenance, impeding the inflowing of the great
central sun. It is true that an elephant never forgets, for
we are the earth's historians. Her biography cannot be
separated from our own, for thus it was ordained from
the beginning. We come to you now to raise your
awareness of the great suffering of this beautiful earth
that we share. Her life hangs in the balance and the
outcome is in your hands. She can become again the
Eden of long ago—a paradise—or she can go the way
of other planets of her kind, becoming dark, cold, and
lifeless orbs circling endlessly through the void of
space.

Our great wild brothers and sisters have failed to
attract your attention, so a few of us have volunteered
to enter your civilization through the darkness of the

circuses, wending our way into positions of influence and visibility to draw your attention once again to the suffering of Mother Earth and all of life upon her. Please listen. We have allowed ourselves to be torn from our mothers' underbellies, to endure indignity after indignity, to be swallowed up in the bowels of depression and despair—all in hopes of finally being heard, not for our own suffering alone, but for the suffering of every sentient creature upon our earth, including those of your own species, who live lives not unlike the most tragic of our own.

Life is a symphony, with each living being contributing its own special note, without which the symphony loses its great depth and beauty. We the elephants sound a deep note, a note so low that those of your species cannot hear it. It is the bass note in the symphony of life around which all other beings sing their own unique songs. We sing this deep note continuously to Mother Earth to balance, soothe, and nurture her. The great whales perform the same function for the oceans of the world, sounding a note of very high frequency that balances and tones the oceans of the world.

If one were to listen from space to the music of earth, one would hear the great low *om* sound of the elephants overlaid with a multifaceted and magnificent symphony of voices and notes of a splendor heard nowhere else in the universe. Captive elephants suffer a great depression from being robbed of their ability to sing their deep note. It takes five of us together in one place to create such a resonance, and often in captivity we are forced into solitary living. We feel not only the deep personal sadness of unfulfilled purpose, but more important, the deep sadness of earth herself as she struggles to shift into a higher frequency of being. In recent years there have been instances of elephants becoming enraged and killing their human keepers. This rage arises from a panic and urgency shared by elephants all over the earth as our numbers are increasingly diminished at the hands of human beings. With increasingly fewer elephants, we are less able to perform our sacred service of ministering to earth as we do constantly. This is what we are here for. Without elephants upon her, Mother Earth will not fare well. Each species of animal serves the earth in a unique and irreplaceable way; each is part of a sacred ministry. Please hear us. The elephants hold the frequency, the framework, in which all of the other animal species hold their own. We speak not for ourselves, but for Mother Earth and all of life upon her.

As Barbara communicated her thoughts and feelings, she began to heal physically and emotionally. Two weeks after our first communication Carol reported that Barbara had trumpeted, perhaps for the first time in her life, and was observed playing joyfully in a mud hole "like a bird at a birdbath." Barbara now lets Carol rub her all over, even the scar around her neck, which no one could touch before. She has developed an intimate relationship with the other elephants at the Sanctuary and has gained much of her weight back. She looks forward to each new day, joyfully anticipating the arrival of two new resident elephants, who will bring their numbers to five, the number required to tone to the Earth.

CHAPTER FOUR

Service

"The purpose of this world is not 'to have and to hold' but 'to give and to serve.' There can be no other meaning."

—SIR WILFRED T. GRENFELL

Several years ago, I attended a writing workshop entitled "Return to Eden: Writing About Animals." Our instructor asked us to think about animals, then discuss what words came to mind. *Noble, peaceful, furry*, and *mysterious* were tossed about the group. Then one woman, in a voice filled with emotion, burst out, "*Tragic!* That's what comes to mind when I think about animals. What we've done to them—how we've enslaved them. *Tragic!*"

We have long been in close relationship with animals. Who

initially instigated the relationship, and whether this relationship has served animals well, is a topic of heated debate. As a
child in school, I was taught that wolves voluntarily took to
hanging around Stone Age fires, seeking warmth and perhaps a
discarded bare bone. Today, as biologists acknowledge the awesome predatory abilities of the wolf, it is considered more likely
that we humans were first to engage the wolf, following them
on their hunts, waiting patiently at their kills for a leftover. In
our earliest years together on earth, surely it is we who needed
animals—for food, for transport, for clothing and shelter, for
protection—far more than they had need for us.

I am deeply humbled when I think about the generous aid
and assistance animals have offered us for centuries. Their
efforts on our behalf are ceaseless, spanning cultures and conti-
nents. In his book *A Perfect Harmony*, Roger Caras writes

> We are the products of the cultures, histories and
> events made possible because there have been animals
> for us to eat, some to milk, still others to wear, ride, and
> otherwise burden. They have been the constants in
> our cultural and intellectual evolution, surpassed in
> importance only by the potential of our own brain.
> And if we have profited hugely from their contribu-
> tions, we surely did not reckon, or care to reckon, the
> price the animals would pay. It all just happened,
> drawing man and animal together until there was no
> way to break free. And that is where we are today. We

are in a partnership far more important in our lives than [we] could have imagined.

Animals are living models to us of service at its most blessed and its most painfully wretched. Acknowledging the full breadth of their service and circumstance can lead us to a difficult moral crossroad. However, difficult crossroads often turn out to be the most fertile fields for soul growth. I could not have said this with conviction before I had cancer, but I can say it easily now.

Few of us who love animals can claim lives utterly free from dependence upon animal service. Those who don't eat animals may wear them. Those who do neither may use products tested upon them or benefit from medical procedures perfected upon them. Because animals are living, feeling beings like ourselves, it is our moral obligation to ask some hard questions. In what situations do we ask or demand too much of animals? Are there instances in which animals enjoy their ministry to us? Are there certain arenas in which we could curb our demands on animals?

In search of answers to these questions, I first wanted to revisit some familiar words. Service, according to the *American Heritage Dictionary*, means "duties performed by a servant" or "duties or work for another." But service is also "acts of devotion to God; witness," and "acts of assistance or benefit to another." Work can mean "activities directed toward the production or accomplishment of something," or "toil . . . drudgery . . . labor."

Exploitation is defined as "making use of [someone or something] selfishly or unethically." Yet a second definition reads: "to employ to the greatest possible advantage." At first glance, these words seem hopelessly jumbled in their meanings. No wonder my own understanding of these concepts has been so clouded. Service covers a broad spectrum of meaning from slavery to altruism. Work encompasses everything from wholesome production to abject drudgery. Exploitation is a blessing or a curse, depending on the circumstance.

These words take on meaning for me in experience and story. My first job as a laundry worker in my late teens was my first experience of work as drudgery. Service was not a word I was willing to apply to sorting and folding hotel sheets. The word *service* came to life for me several years later in the guise of a giant white dog. During this time, I worked at a very small humane society in a rural town. One day humane officers picked up a roaming komondor dog. The beast was the size of a dining room table and completely covered with white hair that hung in ropes or dreadlocks all over his body. Komondors are an ancient breed hailing from Hungary, where they have guarded large flocks of livestock for centuries. It was a rare breed of dog to be roaming any area, and few of us had ever seen such an unusual, magnificent animal.

Although the humane society advertised the dog for several weeks, no one ever came to claim him, so the dog became available for adoption. Local ranchers and shepherds came by to have a look, and several were eager to see if the dog might be a good guardian for their flocks and herds. The shelter, however, had a different perspective on the matter. We did not want animals to be exploited in any way: Our policy was that no animal was to be adopted into any home where it was expected to provide a service or "work for a living." Usually this ruling was enforced when people wanted to adopt "barn cats," whose only source of food would be the mice and voles they could catch. While the shelter's policy certainly protected many animals from abuse, in this case it worked strongly against the komondor, and I was vigorously opposed to it. Livestock guarding dogs are bred and born to serve their flocks and their caretakers. But in the end, the shelter policy prevailed. In a bizarre and tragic turn of events, the komondor was euthanized to prevent this "exploitation."

Twenty years later, I still cannot forget that dog, his comical, rag-mop face, and his quiet dignity as he walked to the euthanasia room. He deserved better. In my younger years, I too had believed that animals shouldn't have to work for a living. They should be loved and supported simply for who they were. (Not coincidentally, I believed the same thing about myself.) Animals, I vowed, should under no circumstance be "worked," misused, or abused.

During my time at the humane society, I could only conceive of this *or* that. The duality of this *and* that was a concept still years ahead of me. I did not understand back then that it is possible to love someone for what they are *and* love them also for the service or work they provide. I never once considered that denying a living being meaningful work could be a form of abuse, too.

One of the oldest service relationships between human-kind and animals is the partnership between shepherds and their dogs. Our farm is surrounded by fields of livestock animals, and several of our neighbors have purchased livestock guard dogs to protect their sheep, goats, emus, and ostriches from coyotes and roaming dogs. It has been a joy getting to know these dogs as they grow from clumsy puppies to serious and devoted guardians. Sandy is a young maremma who watches over a flock of sheep and goats for my veterinarian and neighbor, Mary. Maremmas are an ancient breed of livestock guard dogs from the mountains of Italy. Like many of the old guarding breeds, Sandy is big, white, and fiercely protective. She joined Mary's family when she was a year old. Instantly smitten with Mary's two young daughters, Sandy took longer to learn how to behave correctly with Mary's sheep. At first she would play chase games with them. Then she decided they might be fun to wrestle, and she would show up at the fence line with a smile on her face and thick tufts of wool in her mouth.

On my daily walks with Arrow I would pass by Sandy's territory, and she would come barreling up the pasture, baying at the top of her lungs, her white hackles standing up like pickets on a fence. Only at the last possible minute would Sandy stop, ofttimes crashing into the wire fence like a cannonball. "Wha-roooooof! Wharoooooof!" she would holler viciously while she snapped her teeth and lunged at us. Arrow was terrified. She would scurry behind me until we had passed Sandy's territory.

That first spring Mary lost a tiny lamb because Sandy had been too vigorous in her midwifery. So eager was Sandy to clean the baby and care for it that she trampled it instead. That was five years ago. Mary has lost no lambs since. Sandy has been a wonderful teacher for Mary, who had never "owned" a dog before Sandy:

> I think it was when I took Sandy for her first patrol of the perimeter of her pasture that I felt the first strange tug of a bond between us. With subsequent days, then weeks of going out in the morning to count lambs with her and walk the fence line together, the bond became a partnership—a working relationship reinforced by growing affection and admiration.
>
> Sandy lives in the pasture and shed with the sheep and goats. This is her world, and although she adores visits from her human family, she appears to enjoy her life among her ruminant charges. One big ewe, dubbed Snow White by my daughters, is Sandy's personal favorite. I often see the two of them at rest together, Snow White peacefully chewing her cud while Sandy stands guard at her head. There are those who say it is cruel to let dogs like this live out in the elements when there are warm houses and hearths avail-

able. But I don't think I have misinterpreted the joy and pride with which this animal does her job. For me, a person who may never feel a need to have a dog on my hearth, I can appreciate a partner who shares my interest and protects my investment. I have even felt a special kinship and understanding for the old Basque sheepherder on a PBS broadcast whose eyes welled up with tears as he attested that he could only survive in his profession because of the wonderful dogs who live and work with him.

Sandy has opened my eyes and my heart to the unique realms of relationship between dogs and their owners. I feel she has made me a more sensitive and sympathetic practitioner, and who knows? Maybe someday Sandy in her retirement, or another dog in his youth, will rest in front of my fireplace.

Animals have evolved from their ancient duties of tending flocks to tending people. In the city near where I live, we have a center for the training of guide dogs for the blind. I have never been able to pass a dog and trainer team on the street without feeling tears in my eyes. There is something about the look on the faces of those dogs that touches a place inside me, both nameless and soft. The dogs look up into the faces of the trainers with an expression that seems to ask, "Like this? Am I doing it right? Like this?" Some of the dogs act a bit apologetic, tails low and moving in a slow wag. Some grin ear to ear and prance. Others are serious and dignified in their duties. The focus and intensity of the dogs and trainers is captivating. The partnership appears to be one of mutual respect and, seemingly, of delight. The dogs take to the work. The trainers take to the dogs. The result of the partnership is a circle of service: the trainer's service to the center and to the dogs, the dog's eventual service to her partner who is blind, the sightless person's enhanced ability to serve in his family and community.

I have heard people disparage the guide dog program, saying the dogs work too hard and look tired and sad. I have heard it said that this kind of work is animal enslavement. I disagree. A lot of what the dogs do is wait: wait while their person eats, rides on a bus, studies at school, sits at a work desk. The expression on a waiting guide dog's face can look like sadness. Waiting can indeed be boring. But I've also seen the look of dogs waiting at a kennel for adoption, or waiting on the end of a chain for some small scrap of attention that never comes, or waiting for endless hours while their human companions are away at work.

A dog waiting quietly by her blind partner's side is not a suffering animal. Yes, guide dogs are bred for the work, and in that sense, they are enslaved. But there are shades of gray here. Personally I believe that this is healthy exploitation.

As much as I consider animals teachers and healers, I also think of them as therapists and caregivers. Animals performing this kind of work fall into two general categories: service animals and therapy animals. Service animals are individually trained to perform tasks or to work for a specific person. Guide dogs are the most readily recognized service animals. Therapy animals are an integral part of a treatment plan for an individual or group of individuals. These animals serve many "clients" in a wide variety of social service and health care settings. They offer emotional support, motivation, and a "safe" presence. In all cases, animals selected to serve in these ways must be skillfully and thoughtfully evaluated.

The Delta Society (see the Resources section) has spearheaded an international movement to bring therapy animals of every conceivable kind into hospitals, prisons, convalescent homes, schools, and facilities that work with abused and developmentally disabled children and adults. Animals can work magic in these places, engendering results where conventional methods have failed. So great has been the interest in this new field of study that animals are now training for work in almost any setting you can imagine. In the months and years to come, there will be an increasing demand for people qualified to train service and therapy animals. Already, the number of people and institutions requesting service and therapy animals far outnumber the animals trained and ready to work. For those who love to serve and who love working with animals, this new career is a godsend. Diane Pennington wrote me about her therapy dog, Katie. Her letter epitomizes the tremendous value in this ministry of animals:

Katie is a very special partner with golden red fur and warm, brown eyes. She is a ten-year-old golden retriever with an irresistible personality. As a team, we have been doing animal-assisted therapy for three years. I used to wonder how I could be of assistance to the populations we visit. Now, I simply focus on being aware and staying out of Katie's way as she makes her unique connection with each person she encounters. The "work" is all hers. Katie can soothe and communicate in a way that makes my human speech seem clumsy, limited. Her presence is powerful in its acceptance, intuitiveness, and eagerness to serve. In that way, she constantly challenges my abilities to do the same.

One woman we visited regularly in a mental facility suffered from severe depression and was often withdrawn for long periods of time. Katie was undaunted in the face of such pain, and instead took on just the right qualities to bring the woman out of herself. On one visit, Katie and I respectfully approached her as usual to say hello. She didn't speak to us, so we moved on. Later we came by again, and Katie insisted on sitting by the woman's feet, watching and waiting for a response. When the woman finally looked at her, Katie began to wag her tail and smile her open-mouth dog grin. She leaned against the woman's leg, nuzzling her nose under the woman's hand and inviting pets. Within a few minutes, Katie was lying next to her on the seat, belly up for rubs and pets, and the woman gradually blossomed, then smiled. She began talking about her life while Katie remained there, creating a welcoming space.

Now, this may seem like a simplistic "warm fuzzy," but I know better. Even though our friend was severely depressed and probably medicated, Katie was able to motivate her to focus, to become lucid enough to connect and communicate. Katie got her to move past her sadness and withdrawal long enough to speak with those around her, which, according to the staff, was a significant accomplishment.

Katie's work is profound. She creates a safe, warm, and healing connection with adults and children. She intuitively knows what each needs, enthusiastically gives her energy, and stays until the work is done. Our "clients" receive Katie's gifts easily, whereas they might not be able to receive the same from me or from those around them.

The Delta Society also runs a national center for dispersing information about finding and training service dogs, called the National Service Dog Center. Once utilized only to assist the blind, service dogs are enjoying a career explosion. One organization I know of trains dogs specifically to serve people who have sustained head trauma. Other dogs assist people with seizure disorders. It is believed that the dogs can smell or sense changes in a person prior to a seizure, and will carefully guard their partners during seizure episodes. I have read about dogs who can sniff out cancerous skin tumors, and visited with dogs who care for those confined to wheelchairs.

In some cases, people who have been housebound with emotional disorders have become more independent and active with the help of a service dog. An agoraphobic may find the confidence to leave home with a large, brave canine showing her the way. Those afflicted with panic disorders often find that a service dog can alleviate their sometimes crippling anxiety.

Although dogs are currently the premier service animals, many other species are finding a niche in the service and therapy arena as well. Cats can be wonderful "ears" for a person with hearing loss. Horses are serving thousands in handicapped riding programs. Delta Society has a resident therapy chicken on staff. Rabbits, guinea pigs, and birds are splendid hospital and hospice visitors, and make ideal confidants and companions for abused and at-risk children.

A woman who volunteers each week at a local cancer center with her therapy rabbit, Gonzo, told me about the special gifts Gonzo brings to the hospital wards. One evening this therapy team met a woman who had just had extensive surgery. She asked if Gonzo could visit with her, and Gonzo was placed gently on her chest, where he sat quietly gazing into her eyes for a long time. Gonzo's partner said, "Goodness, he's looking so intently at you! I think if he could speak, he'd have a message just for you." The woman in the bed replied with tears in her eyes, "Yes. Yes . . . he would say that he doesn't care how I look."

Thousand of horses in this country serve in handicapped riding programs. Horses have already done so much for us willingly. Our country grew and expanded on the backs of horses. Our fields and farms flourished under their labor. Now they bring a new healing ministry. The thrill and pride of sitting atop a tall and powerful horse is often a catalyst for emotional and physical miracles. Jackie Malcolm wrote about a handicapped riding program sponsored by her county:

One of our customers was a county-based summer camp for mentally and physically challenged children. After a few weeks of working with each child, we took the kids on a trail ride through the woods. One particular boy, a tall thin six-year-old, had never spoken a word in his life. His body wasn't damaged, but for some reason, he was utterly silent. "Timmy" sat astride a tall, skinny white horse named Casper. During the ride in the woods, I urged the children to stroke their horses and talk to them. Timmy, of course, remained silent. After an hour on the trail, we turned back to the stable. Coming down the last leg of the ride, we passed a green field where the rest of the campmates who didn't care to ride were having a picnic. These children were Timmy's playmates. Imagine our shock and elation when Timmy called out in a loud, clear voice to the campers, "Hi! My name is Timmy and I'm riding Casper!" With that, the child bent forward and hugged the thin white neck of this wonderful animal who had done more for him in one hour than any human had been able to do for him in six years.

Maureen Fredrickson is program director for the Delta Society. Fredrickson has worked with many service and therapy animals and has been particularly impressed with how effective animal therapy programs can be with abused children. She shared two stories that demonstrated an animal's effectiveness in touching people's lives:

Soapy Smith is a twenty-four-pound calico rex rabbit. The rex rabbit's coat lacks the stiff guard hairs of other breeds, resulting in a fur texture that is as soft as a cloud. People look startled when they first touch him and remark at how soft he is. Soapy Smith and I visited a shelter for battered women located in a bedraggled section of the city. The women in the shelter looked at me through downcast eyes. No one smiled a greeting and they appeared disinterested in Soapy's carrier. Everyone seemed tense and ready to flee. One little girl in particular moved like a wisp in the background. Never raising her eyes, never reaching out, she drifted in and out of the gathered group. The staff informed me that she had been there for over a month and had not spoken the entire time. Her mother said she had talked at one time but not in recent memory.

Spreading a blanket on the floor, I sat down and opened Soapy's carrier. As the silent child circled past

me I told the group that Soapy would come to talk to
them if they sat on his towel. Several children did this,
including the silent little girl. In a short time Soapy
emerged from his carrier and slowly hopped from one
child to another. Unlike visits at schools where the
first touches produced squeals of delight, this visit was
unusually quiet. After touching Soapy, these children
looked down and sighed softly or smiled into their
hands. Soapy continued his rounds, and the children
and their mothers gradually began to talk about Soapy
and ask questions. I chatted with the women and children as I kept one eye on the little girl. She sat rigidly at
the edge of the blanket, legs held stiffly out straight in
front of her. She was staring hard at Soapy. It appeared
that he kept making eye contact with her. He would
hop from child to child, each visit taking him a little
closer to the girl. I began to wonder if he was pausing to
give her time to watch him. During all other visits we
had given together in schools, his usual behavior was to
hop around the circle letting each person pet him.
When he got back to me he would wash his face and
then start the circle again. I watched as Soapy finally
worked his way toward the girl. She didn't reach out
to him or encourage him in any way. Rather she sat
tensely, just staring.

Finally Soapy came to a stop about two inches
from her thigh. He quietly reached out and laid his
chin on her knee. I was astonished. While this is a
common behavior for dogs, this is not a behavior

exhibited by rabbits. The child did not reach out to pet Soapy. Instead, she slowly leaned toward him. When her face was within inches of his, she carefully reached out and circled him with her arms. So softly that no one in the room could hear, she began to talk. Folded around the rabbit, she pillowed her head on his back and whispered to him. Soapy remained motionless. I looked up and noticed that the shelter workers had stopped talking. Every adult in the room was frozen into place. Time was suspended. Quietly the child unfolded and sat back up. Soapy sat up, reached forward, and briskly licked her knee. She did not smile. She did not reach out to him, but the rigidity of her back relaxed and her shoulders rounded into a comfortable slope. The little girl stood up and walked over to her mother and began to suck her thumb.

The little girl reappeared when I was preparing to leave. She reached her hands out and looked me directly in the eye. I held Soapy out to her. She wrapped him in a big hug and pressed her face against him. Suspended from my hands as he was, I was concerned that he would begin to struggle. Instead he reached out his head again and laid it on the child's shoulder. His breathing slowed and he closed his eyes. As quickly as it happened, the little girl released her hug and stepped back.

One day a woman and her two daughters came to our farm. The younger daughter was withdrawing from the world. She had begun to stutter, was overly shy, and lacked self-esteem. I took them out to the paddock to meet our horse and donkey. Both animals walked up to us as soon as we entered the paddock. Always looking for carrots or some other handout, Murphy the horse was soon standing over us nuzzling our pockets and hands. Karen hid behind her mother and refused to hold out the carrot. I told Karen's mother to stand still and let them work it out. Murphy did not try to get closer to Karen. Instead, he lowered his head so that his eyes were below her eye level. He then began to make faces at her. He turned his head upside down, rolling it this way and that, waggling his ears from side to side. To add to this undignified display he began to roll his eyes around and hang his lips from his teeth, giving a really foolish grin to his face. Soon we all began to laugh. Karen quickly tossed him a piece of carrot. Without moving Murphy flapped and stretched his lips until he snared the carrot. Chewing slowly with his head still low to the ground, he finished the carrot and then began the show again. After each performance Karen moved a little closer and finally worked her way out in front of her mother. By now Karen's carrots were gone. But Murphy stayed where he was, head low to the ground, reaching his head toward Karen. Gently he moved his head up close and blew softly at her. I told Karen that Murphy really wanted to talk to her. She reached out tentative fingers and Murphy moved his head up until her fingers touched his velvety nose. He froze in place and she began to stroke the edges of his nostrils. He softly exhaled, making a purring sound through his nose. Karen beamed. She walked closer to Murphy and began to stroke his face. Still he never moved.

Karen stepped closer and Murphy lowered his head over her shoulder and, with his head, gently folded her against his chest. He held her there for several moments and then released her. Karen stepped back and smiled up at Murphy. Then she walked proudly back to her amazed mother.

Murphy and Soapy Smith both reached out to interact with nonresponsive people. Soapy displayed behaviors that were very "unrabbit-like," allowing himself to be hugged closely and dangled. Murphy's interest in Karen extended far beyond the carrots she held in her hand. Both animals made gentle and *purposeful* attempts to encourage the children to respond to them. Many domestic animals, including us, seem to thrive on purpose. And many animals, like humans, seem to embody an altruistic spirit. I have always believed that animals are compassionate beings who care about the welfare of others. I am not the only person convinced that animals display compassion and altruism. There has been a surge of interest in this topic in recent years. Author and psychologist Jeffrey Moussaieff Masson explores animal compassion in his pioneering book, *Dogs Never Lie About Love*:

The animal who lives in a community learns the value of helping another individual. Rats are reluctant to press a lever to get food if doing so will also deliver a shock to a companion. They will inevitably press the lever that will not deliver the shock, and some will even forgo food rather than hurt their friends.

Animal communicator Sharon Callahan believes that compassion resides in all living beings and speaks with deep conviction about what she calls "a ministry of animals."

It has often been argued that animals do not have free will, and thus are incapable of true service. Having communicated telepathically with animals since childhood, I can only say that this is not my experience, or theirs. Animals are quite capable of acts of will. We are not the only beings motivated by feelings of compassion and concern for others. Altruism is widespread among animals. Animals have the same innate caring impulses that humans have. They nurture their friends and family members, cooperate for the common good, sympathize with others in distress and perform amazing acts of heroism.... Altruism and service are the instinctive responses of an open heart. In essence . . . all beings come to serve.

I attended a Delta Society conference last year and spent two marvelous days in the company of several hundred service and therapy animal enthusiasts and their working animals. Cats rode by calmly in baskets rigged onto the handlebars of electric wheelchairs. Dogs carried packs, purses, and snack bags for their people. Gonzo, the rabbit, cuddled with me. A parrot rode along on a walker. It was astonishing to see all these animals ushered quietly into restaurants, waiting patiently through hour-long workshops, snoozing through banquet dinners. Their presence was soothing and nurturing.

Of course, there was no end to the stories the conference attendees had to tell. Stories of miracle moments—crippled children who were walking again with the help of a dog, comatose people waking up suddenly when a cat was placed on their chests, battered women reaching out to the halfway-house resident therapy dog for comfort and a sense of safety. At any moment, I expected someone to claim an animal had raised the dead.

At the end of the conference, when I gave the closing presentation to the assembly, I asked how many people had *not* had a "miracle moment" with their animal partner. How many teams had *not* witnessed lame people walking, blind people spontaneously regaining sight, or coma victims suddenly breaking into song? The room went uncomfortably silent. Many hands went up. It is not easy to trust the healing we cannot see with our eyes. Because the medical community in our country has been so very slow to acknowledge the healing benefits of animals, too many people seem to fear that unless their animal partners have made a spectacular, miraculous difference in those they serve, perhaps they and their animals have failed in some way. Short of a media-style miracle with "film at eleven," what proof could these therapy-animal teams offer a skeptical public about the value of their work?

This kind of thinking breaks my heart. We are so conditioned to expect drama and heroics in healing that we forget the staggering importance of all the healing that goes unseen. My own healing from cancer came quietly—a new diet today, a new perspective on my illness the next day, a helpful prayer a week later, the comfort of a new kitten curled and purring cheerfully on my lap the following month. Healing came over time, moment by soft, whispered moment. Healing did *not* come with bells and whistles and a hallelujah chorus. I know that it can. Healing can come in a glorious instant. But it wasn't that way for me.

Often, the healing animals bring comes slowly and gently. To trust in this process takes a certain willingness on our part, a bit of faith. What if we were to imagine that at the end of the leash, in the cat carrier, or on the bird perch sits an avatar, a holy being, a shaman? Imagine that this being can perform miracles of silent, indescribable healing in mysterious ways. Imagine that this being heals by his or her very presence, with a simple look or touch. And imagine you can trust completely that a miracle has occurred each and every time this holy being makes contact with anyone wounded in body or spirit. This being *always* gives exactly what is needed at exactly the right time. What if your job were simply to be the escort of this powerful and exotic healer, to provide a respectful setting where this shaman could work? We may not always trust the work an animal does, but *they* know the value of it. They know they are miracle workers. They often drag their human partners into hospital wards and halfway houses, so great is their enthusiasm.

A special bond exists between a service animal and his human charge. It is a situation where each being contributes something unique to create the whole—the partnership. The partnership then becomes a sort of living entity in itself. I listened to a man paralyzed from the chest down talk about what his service dog meant to him:

> You can't know how afraid I was before Sara was given to me. Sure, I had a specially equipped van that I could supposedly drive, but I was terrified to try. I live alone in the country. What if I dropped the keys? What if I fell out of my chair on the way to the van? I could freeze to death in the driveway before someone found me.
>
> I had no privacy back then. Someone had to be with me in the house nearly all the time. When I'd go out in public, I would see some people actually cross the street to avoid having to look at me. I couldn't get

my clothes out of the closet or pick my shoes up off the floor. Someone had to retrieve the mail and the newspapers for me. I felt helpless and very isolated.

The day I met Sara, all that changed. She is so competent, so incredibly smart. She came to me with a list of words—things she knew how to find and fetch, like keys, bags, papers, or anything I'd drop from my hands. She could turn the lights on and off with a push of her nose. She would work to help me back into my chair if I slipped and fell. Suddenly, we were in the van driving all over the countryside together. Then we went to town. People started approaching us just to greet Sara and ask about her, and I found that people weren't hiding from me anymore. Sara is the best social secretary anyone could ever have! It wasn't long before Sara began learning other words and commands all by herself. Now I feel like I can just talk to her, just have a regular conversation, and she seems to understand exactly what I need from her, sometimes even before I do. She intuits my needs and my moods.

We spend a lot of time alone at home together, and in Sara's presence I never feel lonely. She shines with courage, humor, determination, and acceptance in every waking moment. These are qualities I need more of, and I am learning them from this dog. Sara reminds me to be my best, as she is her best and offers her best in all things. She is a gift of life.

WHILE MOST ANIMALS serve us with their actions, some animals serve us with their lives. The day-to-day life of a livestock animal in an auction yard or a chimpanzee in a research laboratory may be eons away from the life of a hearing-ear dog, but these are animals who serve as well.

Across the road from Brightstar Farm is an eighty-acre pasture where a rancher raises beef cattle for slaughter. The cows stand out in the elements all year long, clipping the clover short and bearing their calves. In winter, the cattle huddle together in a huge circle, heads down, fighting off the sleet and ice storms with the mass of their collective warmth. I pity the ones who stand at the rim of the huddle. In the spring, many calves are born, and depending on their luck, they enter the world on a warm spring day or on a blustery one, exposed to the brutal east wind.

One day I was bemoaning the plight of the cold cows to my editor who lives up the road and has a better view of the pasture than I do. She responded, "Have you ever seen a factory farm? You don't know what misery looks like. On factory farms cows and pigs are warehoused or crated. Some never see the light of day or feel the rain. These cows"—she pointed to the pasture—"are in *paradise*." Her observation brought me up short, forcing me to look at my assumptions and at my less-than-complete thinking. There are many faces of suffering. Often I see suffering where there is little. Sometimes I fail to recognize suffering because I have become numb to it through cultural conditioning. George Bernard Shaw once said, "Custom will reconcile people to any atrocity."

Constantly, I struggle to align my vision and my behavior. I am not yet a vegetarian. Many readers have assumed that I am. I love animals, and currently I eat them. Basically, I do not have a moral dilemma with the notion of people taking the lives of animals for food and clothing. To survive, every living thing is always participating in the death of someone, something. But by purchasing meat at a grocery store, I knowingly fuel the cruel and conscienceless machinery of agribusiness, which I believe is an intolerable, grotesque industry. Writer Alice Walker says that when you eat meat, "You're just eating misery." And in the case of factory farming, she is correct.

In my life, knowledge has been a powerful aid in my decision making. When on the horns of a moral or spiritual dilemma, I frequently turn to books or organizations for information and inspiration. Sometimes I find myself wanting to avoid certain information so that I will not be faced with having to change the way I live. Also, it is hard to read about animal suffering. But it is necessary if we are to make informed, humane choices.

In exploring the moral conflicts of my diet, I discovered several books that gave me a wealth of useful information. *Eating with Conscience: The Bioethics of Food* by veterinarian Michael W.

Fox is a tremendous book that looks openly and factually at the lives of the animals *we* serve—for dinner. In the world of factory farming, livestock animals are defined as food production units. Because my entire personal belief system is based on respectful partnership with animals, this piece of information alone was enough to make me commit to a less meat-based diet. I am also more attuned to supporting the efforts of small farmers who run sustainable farms where animals are treated humanely and lovingly and crops are grown organically with respect for the earth.

Another important book that has shifted my perspective is *Sea Change: A Message of the Oceans* by Sylvia Earle, a biologist and marine advocate. Earle documents the destruction of the seas and the depletion of its fish and marine animals. So alarming is her message and so obvious her passion and compassion for the sea and its creatures that I can no longer pass a fish market without shuddering. *Sea Change* puts faces on fish and personalizes the oceans.

I attended a unique workshop in Northern California called Council of All Beings, which was facilitated by John Seed, an Australian rain-forest activist. Seed offers these councils all over the world (see the Resources section). The intent of the workshop was to give its participants a better sense of belonging *in* the world and *to* the world. Seed explained that the Council of All Beings was developed to "remove the veil of illusion that we are separate from nature." After two days of discussion and group activities, the workshop culminated in the council. For this occasion, each group member created and donned a mask of a being other than human, and spoke for the plight of this being in the council. The power of this workshop, combined with my ongoing reading and soul-searching, has helped me shift to a more plant-based diet, with the goal of becoming a full-time vegetarian.

In exploring the many aspects of animals and service, we sell our souls short unless we also consider the ways in which we might better serve animals. I have received many stories from readers who have devoted years of loving energy in service to their animal partners. One woman wrote to me about ministering to her small crippled dog:

> A nerve disorder rendered his back end totally useless, and we were urged by family and friends to "put him out of his misery." But it really didn't seem to me that Bagel was miserable in the least. His zest for life was fully intact. He just had an out-of-order rear. My husband got busy and built a small cart on wheels. We inserted Bagel into his small chariot and strapped him in. Less than two days later, he was racing around the yard on his front legs, spinning "wheelies" with the cart that supported his crippled hind end.
>
> Bagel needs help relieving himself and often has accidents as he sleeps. We always have cases of paper toweling on hand to keep him and the floors clean. He sometimes gets what seem to be "bedsores" on his para-

lyzed hips, and we rub ointment into these wounds and give him regular massages in the evenings. He loves this special attention! All these little "extras" we do on his behalf are nothing compared to the joy of having him in our lives. He is a constant reminder to us to make the best of life, no matter what the circumstances. Serving him in this way is not a chore or a "waste of time," as others have sometimes thoughtlessly told us—it is our honor.

Rita Reynolds, who helps sponsor an animal rescue organization in her home, has made a commitment to caring for older animals. These elder creatures spend their remaining days in Rita's home and have taught her much about the rites of aging and about the grace of years well lived. She, too, claims that offering service to animals is a joy and an honor. Most people who have chosen to serve animals in some way agree that they gain more than they give by committing to serve.

Still, it is easy for many to benefit from the service of animals while forgetting to ask how we may serve them in turn. I meet with people who have had life-transforming encounters swimming with wild or captive dolphins; unfortunately they don't think to write a letter to their congressman to help preserve these magnificent animals. Many people are eager to tell me of their totem animals—moose, eagle, wolf, otter—and share awesome stories of the power of these animal energies in their lives. I don't know how many of these same people are working to protect these animals and their vanishing habitats, so that their energy can remain on the planet with us. Of the breeders that raise dogs for service work, I don't know how many also donate time to local shelters or rescue services to help ensure a better life for *all* dogs. All of us could commit a little more time to serving the animals who serve us. If we did, the world would be a different place, instantly.

In my struggles to convert to vegetarianism, I have learned firsthand how uncomfortable it is to live a life in conflict with your beliefs. From painful personal experience, I know that when we are able to integrate our ideals and our actions—that is, walk our talk—our souls are better served. The rewards of such wholesome integration include greater self-esteem and an encompassing sense of wholeness. Ironically, in striving to become our most genuine, unique selves, we become more human in heart and more animal in behavior: more honest, more accepting, more "present," and infinitely more courageous.

Over the years I have embraced a word that has helped me marry the contrary and confusing worlds of work/service/slavery/exploitation into a compatible whole. The word is intention, or intent. It means "purpose ... the state of mind operative at the time of an action." In much of life, the alchemical energy of intention determines whether our actions or policies are blessings or curses. If our intention is at all times to promote our own best interests, we can rest assured that other beings will suffer along the way. If our intention is guided by a sincere concern for other beings, including our animal companions, we will do less harm.

Today, despite my intense indoctrination in humane work, I have a bona fide barn cat of my own. Mirella eats dinner on our kitchen counter, but catches dessert out in the barn or in our basement. We love Mirella for who she is *and* for the service she provides. Are we exploiting Mirella because we brought her home specifically for her hunting prowess? Yes, we are employing her to her greatest possible advantage. She's doing what she loves to do.

How can I be sure that we are not misusing her or promoting the continued enslavement and cultural diminishment of animals by "employing" her? There are those who would say that I am demeaning Mirella and abusing mice. To them, I would say that intention is my guide, admitting that sometimes my intentions can be misguided by need or simple naïveté. Still, I depend on intention as my best ally to lead me through the difficult questions to the answers that are right for me. I believe that each person has to make these choices for herself or himself. A refusal to question our actions is the earmark of tragic decisions, both on a personal and a planetary level. But a simple willingness to ask ourselves difficult questions will lead to a path with a humane answer.

Cancer surgeon Bernie Siegel says that to be healthy in

body and soul, we need to pursue our own unique way of loving the world. This is, I believe, the sweetest and highest definition of service: finding our best way to love the world. Many animals serve in this way, and in their enthusiasm and devotion, they can help us find a way to a greater service ethic of our own.

▼ ▼ ▼

Mirella

"You wanna kitty?" Mario waved at the gray tabbies that hurried into the cracks in his great, ancient barn. "I got six, and the mamma, she just drop another eight under my front porch. Mosta those died in the rain last night, though."

I'd been working on a writing project for Mario for some months. He was from the old country and made his own dandelion wine, venison sausage, and cheese from the goats and sheep in his pasture. His wife canned the produce from their enormous garden every summer. Out behind his barn, chickens and turkeys clucked and squawked. "I need lotsa cats on accounta the mice, but I don't need so many!" The kittens, about three months old and as lean as cheetahs, peered out from slats in the loft. "Good hunters," he said. "I don't feed them much, so they gotta be good. You can take any you can catch, but not that little black and white guy," he pointed. "No, he's the one eats sausage right outta my hand." Mario's method of cat keeping was one I'd come into contact with for decades. But time hadn't softened its impact on me: *Too many kitties. Drowned in the rain. Fed infrequently if at all.* It hurt me to even think about it.

Good hunter. A barn cat. In my humane work, barn cats symbolized the worst possible adoptive home for a shelter cat, short of a research laboratory. I can't remember how many people I turned away at the counter who had come for a "good mouser, a barn cat." Nope, nothing to discuss here. No barn cats. The policy was specific and suffered no exceptions.

And now what I dearly needed was a barn cat of my own. Since moving onto our farm and removing all the mothballs and boxes of rodent poison stuffed into the storage spaces in the walls, our house had become a mouse magnet. At night, I could hear them running in the walls and floors: cute, fat, feather-soft gray mice with buff-white bellies and pink ears the size of dimes. Out in our barn, the legions of rodents didn't even bother to run when I came out to feed the donkeys. They would watch me curiously from the rafters and from under and inside the wooden mangers. Bold mice, my neighbor called them. I tried traps a few times, and the results were a horror. Weenie that I am, I wanted a cat to do this work for me. Flora would catch nothing larger or livelier than a moth. Evinrude dabbled at hunting. I knew that the presence of a good, stalking mouser is enough to convince mice to set up housekeeping elsewhere.

Before we go any further, I must tell you that I have nothing against mice, nor do I think they have any less right to life in the divine scheme of things. I am not in favor of eradicating mice from the face of the planet or even from the face of our property. But any animal will protect its immediate den space, and I am no exception. At Brightstar, we needed *fewer* mice, not *no* mice, and I imagined a good hunting cat might be the answer to our prayers.

Every time I am self-righteous about something, my life dishes up a situation where I am forced to come face-to-face with my attitude. And here it was happening again—me standing in a barnyard, rolling down the sleeves of my flannel shirt, taking a piece of sheep cheese from Mario, preparing to grab the first barn kitten I could get my opportunistic hands on.

A small silver tabby with a white bib and white feet inched toward my fingers in a low crouch. She had a funny brown muzzle, like she'd dipped her nose in dirt. She sniffed, I lunged forward and grabbed, and Mirella, the dirt nose, was mine. She cried piteously all the way home and kept up the sad sound while I prepared a large kennel cage for her in the barn. Our house is small, and I didn't think Flora or Evinrude would look kindly upon one more cat face. On top of a bedding of thick straw in the large carrier, I put in a large bowl of cat food, some water, and a small litter box. I thought Mirella could spend a few days in the cage getting acclimated to the sights and smells of the barn before giving her the run of the place. She slunk into the cage, wedged herself along the back side, and looked at me with her ears back and her eyes in accusatory slits. She was angry and shaking.

I returned to the house feeling like a traitor to everything I'd ever espoused about the humane treatment of animals. For the next few days, I performed my barn chores under a suspicious pair of yellow eyes that glared at me from the big kennel up in the hayloft. When I finally let the kitten out, breath held lest she bolt from the building never to be seen again, Mirella left her kennel cautiously, tail up and alert. While I fed and watered the donkeys and scooped up all their old bedding, Mirella sniffed along the corners of the barn with that funny brown nose of hers and skittered across the rafters above the loft. I called to her softly, refilling her food bowl and litter pan. Before I left the barn, she had eaten a full meal and was napping atop her open kennel. The next morning, Mirella was waiting for me in the llama stall, nagging at me for her breakfast. As I filled her bowl, Mirella sat on a storage bin and visited with Phaedra, who sniffed her gently. Mirella was nonplussed and rubbed affectionately along Phaedra's face, her long cat whiskers tickling Phaedra's nose into a boisterous sneeze.

It was that easy. Mirella had staked her claim. The mice started moving out the next day. From what I could observe, Mirella stayed close within the environs of the barn. I would see her sometimes in the pasture, but she was always in sight. When I came out to the pastures, she would run to greet me, sometimes carrying a mouse or a vole as an offering. Soon she took to cuddling with me after I finished donkey chores. When I was ready to go, she would escort me to the pasture gate, but she preferred to venture no closer to the house than that.

Over the weeks, my guilt began to fade, and along with it my staunch belief that the life of all barn cats is so terribly bad. Maybe there was a middle ground I had missed. Mirella clearly loved her barn, her charges, and me. And she loved hunting. She would sit at a mouse hole for hours, tail flicking, eyes fixated on the tiny black entrance.

Through the summer and into a long, colorful fall Mirella kept vigilant watch in the barn. Then, almost without warning, winter struck. It was one of the worst winters on record with ice, snow, and devastating floods. In my cozy bed at night, flanked by two indolent house cats, I would listen to the wind scream outside and think about Mirella out in her hayloft. My old beliefs about the terrible lot of barn cats again loomed up to haunt me. *Poor Mirella*, I thought. *Poor kitty. Cold kitty. Lonely kitty.* Worse, Mirella took to crying mournfully after me when I left the pasture at night after feeding the animals. I'd look back over my shoulder to see her sitting hunched by the gate, eyes imploring and wide, dirt nose twitching, mouth parted in a sorrowful meow.

That did it. All the next week I tried every way I could to coax Mirella into the house. I lured her with food, called incessantly to her from the back porch, even carried her into the living room again and again, only to have her bolt out the door and race across the grass to the barn as fast as her white-booted feet could carry her. It was ludicrous. She began hiding from me, running up into the rafters when I entered the barn. I'm sure she thought I was a lunatic, dragging her from one end of the farm to the other when she knew exactly where she belonged. Discouraged, I gave up trying. I made a concerted effort to convince myself that the barn was a cozy place, which it was, and that Mirella was probably doing just fine, which she was, but I couldn't listen to that fierce night wind without feeling like an utter ogre.

One night in December, I went to bed especially late. The storm outside was so intense I knew I'd never sleep a wink unless I was dead tired, so I watched some late-night television while the wind drove the rain sideways past our living room window. The trees were writhing out in the yard and ice clattered on the metal porch roof. I had moved all the chickens to the work shed earlier that evening. The storm and wind warnings were so bad I had visions of the flimsy henhouse blowing down and chickens hurtling past the window at sixty miles per hour.

With one last guilty look toward the barn, I turned out the porch light and went to bed. Earplugs in position, I fell into a deep, fitful sleep.

Suddenly I was jolted awake. My heart was pounding. Something unfamiliar was on my chest, almost in my face. I could feel fur. *Evinrude?* Evinrude never does a "face thing" at night. For a fleeting, frightening instant I thought it was Ever

Vigilant, the raccoon, come to call through the basement cat door. *No—too light.* Then, by the light of a storm moon, I saw the dirt-brown nose twitching not three inches from my own. A purr, paddy paws on my chest. *Mirella.* Even a barn cat knows when to come in from the cold.

She sniffed my face, licked the crook of my neck, and curled up against me in a tiny, damp ball. A deep sigh, a stretch, soft purr winding down like a slow music box, then silence. I pulled the covers up over her protectively, and we slept like babies.

Chocolate Chelsea: A Canine of Courage

by Patty Aguirre

Words cannot adequately relate the impact that Chelsea has had on our lives. This courageous Labrador was a robust and enthusiastic working dog who lived for the hours spent retrieving sticks from our lake for seven blissful years. Then tragedy struck my gentle friend in the guise of diabetes. While we were working to adjust the amount of insulin she needed, her eyesight began to fail. Her eyes darkened like a foreboding black storm. The storm struck, leaving Chelsea totally blind.

Our friends urged us to be humane and put Chelsea to sleep. Some scoffed at the expense we were willing to accept in order to keep her alive. Chelsea requires a special diet and insulin shots daily. There were days when I wondered if I was being selfish by refusing to consider euthanasia. But then Chelsea would wag her tail with the enthusiasm of a sighted dog, ever-ready should someone stop to play with her. I knew I could never take the life of a being so full of the joy of living!

Chelsea has a physical handicap, and I am a physical therapist. My son has a physical handicap and all my patients have handicaps. Why would I doubt my ability to teach Chelsea to meet the challenge presented by her blindness? I had experience working with blind children, so I understood the basic principles of teaching mobility. I decided to do my best to give Chelsea the opportunity to overcome the roadblock fate put across her path.

My first stop was the toy store. I searched for balls and stuffed animals that made noise. I found a ball that rattled and jingle bells to put inside of whiffle balls. A stuffed animal with a hidden music box was the perfect substitute for Chelsea's silent stuffed bear, which she could no longer locate. Next, I found sugar-free doggy treats at the pet shop to offer her after painful insulin injections. And I tied treats to sticks to aid Chelsea in smelling for them.

The next step involved teaching Chelsea some new commands. "Up" and "down" would be given as a warning for stairs. "Watch out!" became an effective way to warn of an object in her path, such as a tree or parked car. Directional cues included "here," "back," "no," and "there it is." I learned to snap my fingers or clap constantly while walking so Chelsea could follow me or find me. We warn "shot" before giving an injection so we don't frighten her with a stinging surprise. And we avoid rearranging furniture or leaving the vacuum cleaner out.

Chelsea's world is safe again. She still guards her ball and waits in expectation for someone to throw it. She swims in water she cannot see and retrieves sticks with all the ardor of a sighted Lab. She follows me around the yard, successfully navigating obstacles in her path.

Chelsea is an inspiration to me as a physical therapist. If I can modify her environment and teach her new ways of approaching tasks successfully, then I can expect even more from my human patients. She is an inspiration to my son. Shane graduated from college this summer and entered graduate school. As he watches Chelsea struggle to participate in the activities she loves, he is encouraged in his personal struggle to be an active, contributing member of the adult world.

Chelsea brings out the best in all of us. She teaches us to look for the value of life; she helps us look past the physical problems. She is a living example of perseverance. Through her, I have learned new tools to use in my quest to reach people who have given up. Each time she returns from the lake triumphant, dripping wet with a stick in her mouth, I look deep into her vacant eyes and see her lion's heart.

One Soul, Two Halves

by Ellen Urbani Hiltebrand

My husband grew up on a farm where his family raised horses and dogs, so he has spent much of his life in the presence of animals. Yet he nonetheless remarks in reference to Cali and me: "I have never known an animal and a human who were more like two halves of the same soul." Given my adoration of all animals, I had no doubt that Cali and I would become bosom buddies, but here is the story of how I became convinced that some of God's angels wear fur.

I was a Peace Corps volunteer and she a two-month-old ball of matted fur when we met. I decided a German shepherd dog would be a good companion for a single female living alone in a remote village in Guatemala. Big and robust by four and a half months, tragedy struck when Cali stepped on a scorpion ambling across the porch one night. A friend's puppy, two weeks younger, died from the same kind of bite within two hours. While Cali lived, she was completely paralyzed. She could not even move her mouth to eat, so I fed her by dripping raw egg down the back of her throat. Her body deteriorated so much that her coarse hair turned curly from coiling around the bones protruding through her coat. As if that weren't bad enough, she developed a blood infection and a high fever from the wound, so I carried her across the country on rattletrap buses in my arms to an American vet, who put her on IV fluids for a week and then sent us home saying there was nothing more to be done.

Nonetheless, I collected water at night and submerged her in it during the day to control her fever, while soliciting ice from one of the only families in town with a refrigerator. This I tied to her head to keep her brain from boiling. And so we lived for the next month: Me, at five feet three and one hundred pounds, carrying a forty-pound paralyzed dog across my shoulders everywhere I went. Cali and I defied death. We won. She recovered completely.

After that, we were inseparable. Having spent so much time carrying her around with me to monitor her health, I thought it silly to leave her home now that she had gotten it back. She hiked with me through the mountains and curled up under a child's desk each day in the rural schools where I taught. She ate her dinner next to me on the dirt floor each night, and when I went to use the "bathroom" behind a tree, she would squat next to me.

To this day I can think of nothing we would not do for each other. Not that I needed proof of this loyalty, but she demonstrated it one night about a year and a half into my Peace Corps service. By that time, I had moved to a house with an enclosed courtyard and a bedroom that opened directly onto it. The door to the bedroom was made of two pieces of wood arranged in a French-door style. I should have been more concerned with security—a strong wind could have knocked down that door—

but I was due to return to the States in just a few months and had become somewhat complacent. Besides, I arrogantly assumed that because I was young and strong, I could take care of myself in any emergency.

Cali's growls woke me in the middle of that night as she stood guard over me. She was poised on top of the bed facing the door, her teeth bared. Then I heard them: footsteps on the concrete patio outside, slowly advancing toward the bedroom door. Never in all my life had the implications of a sound been more clear to me. Never had I been more terrified.

Although I had rehearsed this scenario in my head countless times—how I would defend myself with quick kicks to the shin and groin and blows to the bridge of the nose—when the moment to act presented itself, I was immobilized by fear. My body was like lead. I could not even move my arm to reach for the knife I kept hidden under my pillow. I just lay there, not even breathing, sure I would suffocate to death before the man outside had a chance to kill me. *Breathe!* I thought to myself, finally managing to suck in a gulp of air. The footsteps echoed closer, and still I could not move.

As he threw his body against the door to break through, Cali leaped from the bed and their bodies hit those two wooden boards at exactly the same time. Through the cracks in the wood, she clawed at him with her paws and slashed at him with her teeth. Still he persisted. Yet every time he stepped back and flung his body at the door to break it down from the outside, she flung her body at it from the inside and held up that rickety old door. After what seemed like an eternity he ran off. We won again.

The more time we spent together, the closer we became, until the similarities seemed almost eerie to those who do not trust in the bonds between animals and the humans they love. Whenever I got a cold, so did Cali. When my allergies got bad after returning to the States, Cali developed allergies too, and after a series of tests, we determined that we are actually allergic to the exact same foods and pollens. When my allergies improved, so did hers. At my wedding, a large outdoor affair, a friend held Cali on a leash throughout the ceremony. Just as the minister asked, "Do you take this man?" and right before I responded "I do," a long, loud howl echoed from the back of the crowd. It was Cali, most surely saying, "I do, too."

Unfortunately, the similarities did not end there. Six months after I was diagnosed with a benign heart murmur, Cali was diagnosed with a heart murmur, too. We were driving cross-country on our honeymoon from Virginia to Oregon with Cali in the backseat. She had developed a weepy eye, and I was concerned some road dust was irritating it, so we stopped at a veterinary hospital in Salt Lake City to have it checked. The vet looked at her eyes, then as part of the routine exam put the stethoscope to her chest. His forehead furrowed and he bit his lip as he moved the stethoscope across her body for a full five minutes. Finally he straightened up and addressed us. "Her eyes are fine," he said, "but she has a horrible heart condition." As I held her and cried, the vet took an immediate ultrasound to confirm his diagnosis: subaortic stenosis. There was nothing to be done; the cardiac specialist said he had never heard a worse heart. "If you treat her normally, she has two months to live," he said. "If you keep her inside at all times, keep her from running around or exerting any energy, she may live for up to two years."

"I can't do that," I said. "She plays outside every day; we run together all the time. She'd be absolutely miserable locked up inside."

"Then you'll kill her."

"Then she'll die happy," I retorted. I knew she'd prefer a short, happy life to a long, miserable one, and I relished the opportunity to ensure that the end of her life was as much fun as the beginning had been.

That trip to the vet was well over four years ago. Cali and I walk or jog a couple of miles to the park every day—depending on my level of stamina—where she plays with a pack of dog friends and swims in the river. She has traveled back and forth across the country two more times, hiked the redwood forest, and is so healthy that the only reason we go to the vet anymore is to update her vaccines. Her heart is still in terrible condition. In fact, whenever we do go to the vet, the staff always politely asks if everyone in the office can listen to it. "You'll never hear a heart like this again," they say to one another. The vet admits he has never seen a healthier-looking dog with a worse heart, and adds that there is no medical explanation for her longevity.

I can explain it, though. Cali teaches me every day that there are forces greater than medicine and technology. From the minute she recovered from that scorpion bite, she has repaid my nurturing with unwavering loyalty and friendship. She has been the guardian of not only my physical body but also my soul. In times of loneliness and fear she has again and again offered herself wholeheartedly and unselfishly to me. Out of love for me, she continues to live. I am no fool; I know that eventually Cali will die. Nonetheless, I win again. I have had the opportunity to share my soul with a wise and generous teacher. When I needed it most, God sent me an angel disguised in fur to remind me of the power of love.

CHAPTER FIVE

Messengers, Dreams, and Visions

"It's not the surface work that's needed now.... It's the deep work. We need to bring our dreams and visions down to earth and put them into our lives. In my country we can't just stagger around in our visions—the rattlesnake teaches us that. We need to be awake and pay attention to where we put our feet."
—NATIVE AMERICAN ELDER,
from *The Feminine Face of God*
by Sherry Anderson and Patricia Hopkins

I have rarely found moments of great insight and wisdom in lectures, textbooks, or lists of facts and figures. When my soul chooses to speak to me, it is most often in dreams, imaginings, unlikely "coincidences," and symbols or metaphors. Animals populate these ancient regions of knowing. Before spoken words and alphabets, humans and animals were in relationship with each other. For thousands of years, humans turned to animals in song, ceremony, dance, and vision quest for guidance and wisdom. While our civilized minds may have forgotten these ways of knowing, our spirits have not forgotten our animal messengers and mentors.

Animals who live in our dreams, visions, and imagination have as much wisdom and healing to bring us as the animals who live in our physical reality. Animals can come as messengers, bringing a flash of insight, hope, or clarification. When I was still naturally steeped in magic as a child, I knew these things intuitively. But as I grew older, I lost the knowing. When I was challenged with cancer, I learned to erase the boundaries between physical and mystical realms, between what is seen with the eyes and what is seen with the heart. Now I no longer make many distinctions between the value of inner and outer experience. Gratefully, I have been able to reclaim some of the enchanted awareness I had as a child.

In *Animals as Teachers and Healers*, I wrote about my use of a totem animal—Gaia, a large wolf—to help me visualize healing from cancer. Three times daily, I would imagine Gaia and her pack racing along my blood system, gobbling up cancer cells. Using that vision that had become so meaningful to me through my daily practice, I boosted the number of fighting immune cells in my system by 20 percent in just six weeks. My doctors were overjoyed. Gaia is an animal who lives only in my heart. It has been ten years since my cancer journey, yet I still visit with Gaia frequently in my thoughts. She has become as real to me as any other animal that lives with me at Brightstar Farm.

Many of the most profound animal-related stories of my life defy physical reality. One could easily write them off as "meaningless coincidences." In the past, I was reluctant to share many of these stories for fear of ridicule. How could I explain to a skeptic that I saw a red-shafted flicker at my bird feeder for three days in a row, and that it had a fantastic message for me about coming good fortune? Or that a snake on my porch brought me some important insights about my relationship with my stepson? Or that my dreams about bears taught me about time management?

If people look at me strangely when I share a particularly uncanny or seemingly "coincidental" story about an animal, I laugh and tell them what cancer surgeon Bernie Siegel told an audience full of cancer patients. Siegel said that we could spend the rest of our days on earth waiting for the meaning of life to come knocking at our doors, or we could create meaning right now by choosing to see it in our everyday experiences. Siegel believes that the *true* meaning of life is the depth of meaning we assign to it. He teaches people that the sublime, the ridiculous, and even the most trivial moments of our lives offer us an opportunity to build meaning in a way that is uniquely and vitally *us*. Ram Dass, who lectures extensively on the process of healthy aging, states this same concept a bit differently: "The quality of our life experiences is dependent upon our perspective on them." My husband has another perspective: "Some people say *coincidence*. I think a better word, really, is *providence*."

Our lives will never be more or less meaningful than we envision them. Our experiences are no better or worse than we perceive them to be. Intuitively we know this. Otherwise phrases such as "One man's trash is another man's treasure" or "One's heaven is another's hell" wouldn't have embedded themselves in our culture. Perception is everything.

Cynicism, sarcasm, rigid skepticism—these are approaches one can take in attempting to cope with the more unusual experiences of life. But they will not fill us with insight or allow us to feel the sweet touch of enchantment. Instead, these negative approaches to life diminish its wonderment and fullness. My approach to interpreting the moments of my life might seem fantastical and unlikely to those with a more technical grounding. But I will stand on my ground gladly and with no apology. Unequivocally, I believe in the validity of my personal experience, and what truths those experiences hold *for me*. My experiences have taught me where it is best for me to stand and what ground supports me securely and lovingly. More than religious doctrines, current trends, political correctness, or the scientific method, I trust what *life* has taught me.

When I share my stories about animals, I am amazed at how creatively these stories are interpreted by those who hear them. Each person may draw a completely different meaning from the same story. A young man at one of my workshops spoke about two boisterous raccoon kits who had been visiting his backyard every evening. When one kit was fatally struck by a car in front of his house, its companion pulled the broken body to the side of the road and sat there all evening, touching the dead kit and chirring to it softly. Some listeners believed the story was about the universal nature of grief. Others said it reminded them to treasure their friendships. Still others felt the story spoke to them about the need for closure at death, and the value of spending time touching and grieving over the physical body. This was simply a story about a raccoon that died, yet it was rich in meaning.

The meaning each person brings to an experience reveals a great deal about that person's approach to life. While I was explaining this concept at a lecture recently, an elderly man with a huge grin and a wild mane of white hair called out, "Yes! By their stories ye shall know them!" People who imbue their lives with enchantment and meaning, who choose to imagine that the universe is sending loving messengers to them, and who see experiences as rich with possibility are more likely to satisfactorily deal with the myriad twists and incomprehensible turns that are a part of everyone's life. Simply put, these people have a bigger tool box to work with.

I believe that most of us seek guidance for our journey through life. Putting aside preconceived notions about where guidance may dwell, we will at once find it everywhere: in the trees who show us the value of bending and of firm roots, in the sight of a hawk snatching up a songbird and teaching us about clear vision and death. Animals are, of course, only one kind of messenger, but I look to animals because my attention and my passion are with them. My husband is captivated by sound, music, and motion, and I suspect that inspiration comes to him most easily on that path.

Through my experiences with Gaia, I began opening myself to other animal guides and totems. Many times a week, I spend quiet moments of reflection in the quiet beauty of our yard or before a lit candle in my writing office. Sometimes I meditate. Often I just close my eyes and ask for guidance. Messengers have come in mental visions, and some as actual animal visitors to Brightstar Farm. I have learned to watch closely during the day for unusual encounters with animals. Perhaps a new bird begins to frequent our feeders or I see a particular wild animal several times over several days; perhaps an animal approaches me in a new way or I see a dramatic or unusual encounter between two animals. I make note of all these. If I dream about animals, I write the dream down.

Living in the country, I see many different animals every day in addition to my animal family. Birds, squirrels, mice, voles, moles, frogs, foxes, and coyotes cross my path. I do not consider all of them messengers. The decision to acknowledge a particular animal in that way comes as a "felt sense" in my body. It has taken me a long time to become aware of this subtle sensation. The best way I can articulate it is to say that certain encounters with animals trigger a sense in me of "Oh, yes...pay attention here." It is a feeling I have had to learn to trust. For help in translating messages from animals, I turn to guidebooks of totem animals or to quiet reflection and try to decipher what insight that animal may have been leading me to.

Digging in the garden last spring, I uncovered a sleeping garter snake. It raced away from my spade into the periwinkle in a flash of black and yellow striping. The following day as I headed for the henhouse to gather eggs, another garter snake slithered across my path. Later that same afternoon, I sat on my back porch with a tall glass of iced tea to do some hard thinking about my stepson. He was living with us, and I was not adjusting well to his teen years. I took most of his mood fluctuations personally: the posturing, the defiance, the selective hearing. It was all aimed, I imagined, at me. Sipping my tea while working myself into a state, I suddenly noticed a flutter of motion low and off to my left. Looking down, I saw a garter snake carefully lifting itself through a crack in the boards of the deck. I gasped in surprise. The deck is raised a good eight inches from the dirt beneath it. The snake had periscoped its slender body straight up past that height to reach the crack by my foot. As I watched, the snake pulled its entire body onto the deck, slid across my foot, and curled up near a pot of cactus about two feet from where I was sitting.

Putting aside my tea, I hurried to my bookshelf and took down my set of Animal Medicine Cards. Looking up "snake" in the medicine cards guidebook, I read: "The transmutation of the life-death-rebirth cycle is exemplified by the shedding of the snake's skin. It is the energy of wholeness. . . . If you have chosen this symbol, there is a need to transmute some thought, action, or desire so that wholeness may be achieved . . . remember, magic is no more than a change in consciousness." I thought about my stepson, who was experiencing the physical change from childhood into the rebirth of his "adult skin."

The more I sat with the image of the snake, the more I realized that the anxiety and anger I was feeling toward my stepson were of my own making. If I could transmute my perceptions about him, I could choose to view his behavior in an entirely different, less personal way. The snake reminded me that the power to transform my thinking is always in my hands. Something subtle in me shifted that afternoon, and I was able to view my relationship with my stepson differently. No longer did I feel he was aiming anything at me. No longer did I feel the need to defend myself against his growing pains. My image of him transformed. The garter snake had brought me an important, healing message.

When my first book came out, I worried about claiming the title of author. "What is an author supposed to act like?" I asked myself. "How does one adopt a new role in life, and how does that new role blend with the others: wife, daughter, country girl, manure scooper?" This was a new and foreign role and I was nervous about going on book tours and speaking to people. It was no coincidence that Ever Vigilant the raccoon made his first appearance at our farm during this time. I found him in the maple tree one evening as I went to lock up the chickens for the night. He was perched in the crook of the trunk, all bunched into a large, fat ball of smoke-colored fur. His striped tail, thick and luxurious as a feather boa, hung down easily within my reach. Black eyes reflected from an even blacker face mask. He sat like the Cheshire Cat in *Alice in Wonderland*. I left a thick chunk of corn on the cob at the base of the tree for him, and the next morning it was gone. At midday, I heard Arrow barking in a frenzy and went out to find Ever Vigilant peering down from the skinny limb of a Douglas fir. Arrow treed the raccoon several more times that week. When I looked up "raccoon" in *Animalspeak* by Ted Andrews, I read the following:

> One of the most striking features of the raccoon is the mask it wears.... Concealed behind a mask, people could become something or someone else. We can become whatever we want by wearing masks.... Raccoon medicine can teach you how to become dextrous in the masks that you wear. It can show you how to wear a healing mask or show you the face you shall become. The raccoon holds the knowledge of how to change our faces.

Instantly, I understood that Ever Vigilant had come to show me a creative way that I could grow into my "author skin." I could imagine that I was putting on a mask, my author mask. For the time being, I did not need to worry about completely absorbing that new role in my life. It would come over time ("the face you shall become"). Meanwhile, I could simply put on my author face and play the part as needed. I chose to believe that Ever Vigilant's visit was a gift from the universe to me, sent through one of earth's many talented and generous message carriers. A friend once told me, "Sometimes the fingerprint of God is a pawprint." And sometimes the voice of God is carried on the back of a silver-smooth snake or in the delicate mask of a fat raccoon.

GIFTED WITH WINGS to carry them to the heavens, to the gods, or to the "sky people" of our native cultures, birds have been hailed as message carriers throughout oral and written history. Doves are said to bring peace, the owl death and rebirth. The raven is known to be a cross-cultural bearer of magic. At a book reading one evening, artist Susan Seddon Boulet approached me and said, "Do you know, sometimes a bird can give its very life for you?" Then she told me her story.

Years before, Boulet had been diagnosed with breast cancer, and although her life had been steeped in shamanic tradition and faith, she was apprehensive about death. "I have my doubts, like most people must have. Is there anything waiting for us when we die? Sometimes I know there is, but then doubt creeps in," she confided. One afternoon as Boulet was driving toward home, she noticed a large hawk sitting by the side of the road. It didn't fly off as she sped by, and she watched in horror as the car behind her slammed into the bird, sending its body spinning off the road in a cloud of feathers. Boulet pulled her car over and raced back to the bird, who was "mortally, mortally wounded." Gently she scooped up the stricken creature and wrapped it in a cloth. Its wings were broken. Blood seeped from its nostrils. "The hawk was dying. I felt that the least I could do was to take it home and pray for it," Boulet explained.

In her home, Boulet sat with the injured hawk, crying for its pain and praying for death's release. Suddenly the bird's lemon-yellow eyes sprung open. It peered intently at something over Boulet's shoulder. In the next instant, the hawk leaned forward and spread out its wings into a full and magnificent fan—wings Boulet knew were shattered. Eyes still fixed over Boulet's shoulder, the hawk flapped its wings, determined to fly toward whatever had captivated it so completely. Once, twice the massive wings pulled up, then swiftly down. On the second downbeat, the wings collapsed, the head folded forward, and the bird was dead. Boulet sat in silence for a long time holding the hawk. "I knew instantly what that bird had seen over my shoulder," she said. "Death had been sitting there for some time, you know, and the hawk had seen it. *And moved toward it.* With its last breath, the motion was forward. And that gave me great strength."

Susan Seddon Boulet passed away a year after she told me

this powerful story. I believe the yellow-eyed hawk was waiting for her.

IN THE SPRING OF 1996, I saw a large female flicker at our bird feeder. Flickers normally eat insects, so I was surprised to see her at the seed bin, but her appearance delighted me. She was a stunning bird, flecked with river-stone colors. A jet-black crescent moon rose beneath her buff-and-black-spotted throat. On her head was a bright red feather cap. When she flew, the undersides of her wings flashed a brilliant scarlet. The flicker's arrival in my yard would drive all the smaller birds away. She was nervous at the feeder, weaving her head from side to side, alert and on constant guard. One move from me would send her high into the maple tree, then off across the back pastures. The only creatures who could move without startling her were the chickens, who lurked beneath the feeder and loved the fact that she scattered seeds everywhere.

She appeared at the feeder every morning for several days. Toward the end of the week, I recognized that body sensation that says, "Oh yes, pay attention here." So I looked up "flicker" in *Animalspeak*: "When the flicker comes into your life, it will reflect new bounding leaps of spiritual growth.... Your physical and material life are going to change.... The stimulation of latent talents is going to be a catalyst for major creative changes in your life. Flicker indicates a time of rapid growth and trust." Everything I read about the symbolism of the flicker was good, invigorating, and exciting. I lived with the happy anticipation of something wonderful on my horizon, confident that the flicker was a messenger for me.

Early the following week, I learned that my book *Animals as Teachers and Healers* had been sold to a large publisher. My life and fortune began changing rapidly. Thanks to the flicker, the news of the sale came not as a surprise but as the eagerly anticipated opening of a new life-path. I trusted that the sale of the book would be good for me and my family, because the signs surrounding the event had been so positive.

It has been said that when an animal—living or dream—chases us or leaves its mark with tooth or claw upon us, that animal is a messenger of the most powerful magnitude. When an animal encounter leaves us breathless or wounded, we are being asked to look closely at some issue in our lives or at some power we have not been willing to claim for ourselves. In certain indigenous cultures, an animal who touches you, marks you, or challenges you is giving you its power. If you survive the encounter, this animal spirit will be your ally for life.

Tamara Leibfarth shared a story she had written about a close encounter she had with a grizzly bear in Denali National Park and of the "marks" he left upon her. Leibfarth and a friend were hiking deep in the back country of the park to take photographs of the abundant wildlife. Hiking near the Toklat River, her friend turned and said, "There's a bear in the tundra over there." Leibfarth quickly took some pictures of the young grizzly bear with its head stuck in some berry bushes. Wise to the ways of hiking in bear country, she and her friend called out, "Hey, bear!" to announce themselves to the grizzly, who never bothered so much as to glance their way. Leibfarth continues:

> We wanted to walk to the river valley, but we also wanted to avoid the bear, so we began walking around her above the river. I slipped on some loose gravel by the edge of the embankment and slid to the bottom, laughing. When I pulled myself to my feet with the help of my friend, the grizzly walked out of the tundra toward us and stopped about fourteen feet away. Time stood still. She cocked her head. I saw a look of amazement and curiosity on her face. My friend linked her arm through mine and we slowly began waving our free arms to look as big as we possibly could. We backed away, saying, "Hey, bear," and whatever else came to mind that seemed appropriate.
>
> The bear moved forward and we stopped. I felt a calmness settle all around me. Reaching for my camera, I took a picture of the bear as she lumbered toward us. My friend's voice took on a fearful edge, and I heard her asking, then begging this bear to please just go away. "Don't make eye contact," she said, but the bear was so transfixing, so mystical, so beautiful, I couldn't help but look at her. I met her eyes, she

cocked her head. How drawn I felt to her! Breaking eye contact, I stood quietly with my friend beside me.

Slowly the bear approached me and sniffed my left knee and foot. Again, she cocked her head. Then while I watched, with breath held, she reached out very slowly with her left paw, and gently laid it on my foot and pulled it toward her. Her claws were brown and as long as spikes. My friend grabbed my arm tighter, and we both told the bear insistently to go away. I relaxed my leg and watched it spring back against my body, and the bear jumped back in surprise. We had food in our day packs. The bear began to circle us, confused, as though she didn't know quite what to do next. My friend picked up a rock and threw it at the bear, shouting at her to leave. I picked up rocks, too. We pelted the bear with stones and shouted and finally, thankfully, she ran back toward the river.

We hurried back to the ranger station and told them about our encounter. I was shaken and breathless, trying hard to stem the adrenaline coursing through me. How ordinary I made it all sound, like bears just walk up to people all the time. The ranger told us that, based on our description of the bear, it was probably about three years old, the "teenage" years for bears, when they get boisterous, curious, and into trouble.

As the weeks passed, I reread my journal often to remember that amazing day. Watching TV specials about grizzly bear encounters, my friend and I realize how lucky we were. Each time I tell the story to someone, it becomes more powerful, more special, more real. "Why us?" I ask myself. "Why were we so lucky and so privileged to experience such a magical encounter?" Only the Great Sacred Mystery knows. I look at my photos of the bear and touch the three deep scratches on my left hiking boot. I could have reached out and touched her that day. What powers were looking over us and protecting us as we faced our fears and danced with the bear that day?

Our dreams about animals can offer tremendous insight and guidance. Writer and dreamworker Rhianon Haniman believes that animals in dreams can be "absolutely trusted." The challenge for most of us is getting a grasp of what the animal messenger is saying to us. "The road that has always been open to that place of wisdom is the dream," writes Haniman in the *Dream Network Journal*, "and the more we pay attention to our dreams, the more our unconscious responds with ever more vivid and elaborate imagery. If an animal speaks to us in a dream, we do well to listen."

For years, I had a recurring dream about bears chasing me up trees, up curtain rods, up flagpoles, up whatever. I would climb in a panic far above the bears while they drooled and snarled below and snapped at my dangling feet. These bear dreams were exhausting, and I would awaken from them frazzled and more tired than when I went to bed. One day I was trying to describe the dream to a friend, and I heard myself say, "It's like trying to rise above the bears." My friend answered, "Oh, like rising above the things you cannot bear?" That easily, she had brought me the key to the dream. Looking back in my dream journal, I saw that these dreams always came to me when I was struggling along with too much on my daily plate, too much on my mind, or too much in my heart. This dream was a reminder that I had taken on more than I could bear. And that I needed to find a way to rise up to the occasion. Now, whenever my nighttime bears lumber in, I take a close look at my work schedule and start managing my time more carefully, leaving room for an afternoon nap, a walk, or more time to visit with my animal family.

Sometimes dreams come to us early in our lives and hold fast on to us. Daniel Quinn, one of my favorite authors, had such a dream. I first discovered Quinn through his award-winning novel *Ishmael*. His book unveils a new and thoroughly absorbing story of human history, as told through the eyes of a gifted teacher—an ancient lowland gorilla named Ishmael. The book is filled with such visionary ideas. I found myself wondering how Quinn was able to write such an unusual and honest work.

In his autobiography, *Providence*, Quinn describes two events that shaped his destiny and brought *Ishmael* to life. One was a dream he had when he was six. In this dream, young Quinn is walking home one night from a movie when he finds his way blocked by a huge fallen tree. A large beetle comes scurrying down the trunk of the tree and speaks to him. "It's all right," the beetle reassures the startled youngster. "Don't be afraid, I'm not going to hurt you. I only want to talk to you." The beetle tells Quinn that he is needed somewhere. Quinn is transfixed. *Where?* The beetle points solemnly toward a lovely forest at the edge of the sidewalk where a deer stands motionless, looking at the young boy. "You need to know some things, you see, if you're going to help us," said the beetle. "It will almost mean giving up your life, will almost mean becoming one of us. . . . We need to tell you the secret of our lives." Without a moment's hesitation, Quinn steps off the sidewalk to follow the deer—and wakes up, heartbroken and sobbing that he had not been allowed to enter the forest. In *Providence,* Quinn says of the dream:

> How deeply I accepted this six-year-old's dream as a description of my destiny. From that age, I knew that, somehow or other, I would make the dream come true—or rather, that I would finish it. I hadn't been allowed to finish it as a child—and this is exactly how I understood it at the time. I knew its fulfillment was something that was to happen later. The purpose of the dream was to plant in me a lifelong yearning for its fulfillment. Someday I would be allowed to step off that sidewalk and enter another world.

Just before I began working on this book, I had a dream about a mother wolf and her pack of cubs. I had been feeling very apprehensive about writing a second book. The excitement of my first book project gave me a rush that propelled me through the initial draft and many extensive rewrites. In facing the second book, doubts and fears replaced the adrenaline. "What if I already said all there was to be said about animals as teachers and healers?" I asked myself. The wolf dream was my answer.

In my dream, the wolf mother brought her cubs into a dorm room where I was staying. I was seeking help to have the cubs and mother collected and taken safely back to the wilderness. When I awoke, I read all my guidebooks. This is the piece from the medicine cards that said *yes!* to me: "As you feel wolf coming alive within you, you may wish to share your knowledge by writing or lecturing on information that will help others better understand their uniqueness or path in life. It is in the sharing of great truths that the consciousness of humanity will attain new heights." When I read that paragraph, I knew that I would find much more that needed to be said, and that this second book was indeed ready to be born.

Sometimes animals who have died return in dreams to comfort and reassure their human companions. These experiences are far more common than I originally imagined. I have received dozens of stories about these special dreams, all relating a tremendous sense of peace and joy that came on the wings of these visitations. One woman, Willia Mather, wrote to me from central Mexico about a dream she had nine days after the death of her white German shepherd, Sookie:

> The native people here have a ceremony on the ninth day after a person's passing. That night Sookie showed up in my dream and lay down beside me in a way she had never done before. I put my arm around her. I can still feel her long velvet fur in my hand. She spent the whole night with me. The next day I felt so at peace. At first I felt that it was my private gift from Sooki, but I knew I would eventually want to share it, and that time has now come.

I believe our animals sometimes return to us after death in the bodies of other messenger animals. Sophie Craighead wrote me about an experience she had with a raven shortly after her beloved golden retriever, Rocky, died. She said that ravens often came to her during times of great difficulty or change:

> Rocky was my guardian angel, seeing me through some of the toughest physical and emotional challenges of my life. Three days after he died, I went cross-country skiing up Shadow Mountain with my remaining canine family. There were three inches of

fresh snow and I was the first to break the trail. It was one of those magical Jackson Hole days when the sky is brilliant blue and the snow glitters like diamonds.

As I started to go up the hill, a raven circled my head really low. He almost landed on my shoulder. Then he went about thirty feet up the trail, perched in a tree branch, and waited for me. When I got there, he flew another thirty feet or so up the trail. This happened all the way up to the top of the lookout spot, where I stopped to say a prayer for Rocky. As I was praying, the raven began circling over my head again, and my dogs began barking wildly. The raven turned, dipped a wing at me, and flew away. I just know that raven was Rocky, coming to let me know that he was fine, free from pain, and that he could still visit me in this special way.

A friend of mind, Parris, told me about a special dog who guided her to her dream home. Parris once lived in the woods of Southern Oregon. From her bedroom window, she would occasionally see a beautiful white female German shepherd peering at her from the trees at a distance. None of her neighbors owned a dog like this, and Parris never saw the dog during any of her many walks around the neighborhood. Only in those misty morning hours would she see her, standing white and still against the dark of the green trees. Because of the dog's coloring, Parris knew she was a domestic animal, but there was something about her pose in the woods that made her seem wild and free. The image of wildness stayed with Parris, and she began to think of the white shepherd as a symbol of freedom. Then Parris moved to Portland.

Parris and her family lived in a home in a suburban area near the city for a while, but she and her husband were always looking for the perfect piece of land farther out in the countryside—a place close to trees and water where they could live and grow. One day as Parris and her husband were looking at a piece of property on the banks of the Willamette River, Parris looked over her shoulder. And there she stood on the edge of the lot, gazing fixedly at Parris—a beautiful white German shepherd. Without hesitation, Parris bought the lot. She learned that the white dog lived just next door to the property. During the four years it took Parris and her family to build their dream home, the white dog would appear every time they visited their building site. Shortly before Parris and her family moved in to their new home, the white dog became sick and died. "It was as though her mission had been completed," said Parris. "That was two years ago, and I am waiting to see her again, to guide further dreams."

In her book *The Secret Language of Signs*, Denise Linn writes about a man deeply depressed over the loss of his wife, desperate for some sign that death didn't mean the utter end of her—body *and* soul. He finally asked his wife to please send him a sign that would let him know she was okay. The next morning the man awoke to a brightly colored blue jay tapping insistently on his window. Blue jays had always been his wife's favorite bird. She had even told him a story once about a blue jay that used to tap on the window of her childhood vacation home each morning. "As soon as I saw that blue jay pecking at the window, I knew it was a sign from Ruby," said the man. "I knew she was all right. After that, I felt the heavy sadness that I had been carrying around with me just lift."

A reader sent me a story about feathers that signaled her lost cat's return home:

> Our cat, Samuel, failed to return home one evening. By the next morning, we couldn't help thinking the worst, especially when we saw vultures hovering overhead. That evening, after a daylong search, we came across two brown and orange feathers. My fiancé remarked to me how uncommon it was to find two such clean feathers. He initially decided to place the two feathers in the web of his dream catcher. Instead, he placed the two feathers in Samuel's bed. "Maybe these feathers will catch Samuel for me," he said.
>
> The next morning as I was brushing my hair, in walked Samuel, tired and shaking. We could see that he had been attacked by some animal, as he had puncture wounds that demanded immediate medical attention. Afterward, we watched as Samuel went directly to his bed to lay down. There upon his bedding rested the two feathers nestled on an oak leaf!

The two feathers had found Samuel and brought him home.

To downplay the importance of these intriguing stories of visions and dreams is a surefire way to block out huge portions of the knowledge and healing that the universe has to offer us. If animals are, as Carl Jung suggests, archetypal images in our dreams that speak to emotions universal throughout human-kind, then we would do well to heed his advice to listen to their voices. But if animal dreams and visitations are merely brain blips of our sleeptime or an occasional odd coincidence, then their meaning lies, as Bernie Siegel suggests, in our own hands.

▼ ▼ ▼

The Deer, the Coyote, and the Hawk

Teton Canyon, Idaho, is dazzling any time of the year, but most so when it lies under thick quilts of snow. Many times, I had roamed the canyon when I lived just over the hill from Teton Valley in Jackson, Wyoming.

Arrow, Lee, and I were returning to Oregon from a book-research trip to Yellowstone, and Lee had been eager to spend the last day of that year's ski season at Grand Targhee, just a few miles up the road from Teton Canyon. With a long day in front of us, Arrow and I—poor skiers at best—decided to visit my old hiking ground. I had not seen the canyon in twenty years, and I was glad to find it so little changed in all that time. In wandering through Yellowstone with its groves of white aspens and creeks red with willow bushes, I found myself at once exhilarated and homesick for these mountains that had been home to me many years before.

"Home. What is home, anyhow?" I asked myself as I wandered along the mountain path. Home was my farm, plush hillsides of near-blinding green. Home was Oregon rivers guarded by stands of gray alders and salal bushes, and wind that blew down the Columbia Gorge turning my ears to frozen red cubes. I loved my home in Oregon and yet had never fully let go of a longing that nipped at my soul whenever I remembered the days of my young adulthood in the Rocky Mountains. Over the years, I continued to refer to the Tetons as my spiritual home. My seven years in the Rockies played out over and over again in frequent dreams of old friends, brittle sagebrush, and summer thunderstorms that wailed down the mountainsides.

As Arrow and I headed up the narrow path that disappeared into Teton Canyon, I was lost in questions about the meaning of home. *Home. Homesickness.* Together we walked through stands of lodgepole pines bent with snow, over meadows with streams gurgling under a cover of winter powder, among white-barked aspen groves. At the edge of a stream bank I dusted snow off a boulder that looked like a protruding belly and climbed on top to sit and daydream. The stream was narrow and champagne clear, its waters reflecting the coffee-brown color of last autumn's leaves, which still lined its banks and bottom. An ancient cottonwood reached overhead, bare branches poking inquiring fingers into a sky that flipped from cobalt blue to graphite gray as snow showers came and went. I sat on my boulder and thought about home. The home I knew in Oregon, the home I remembered in Wyoming. And I thought about homesickness and wondered why it stung me so keenly that afternoon.

Images of Yellowstone and the thousands of animals we had seen drifted through my thoughts. We would round a crook in the road and come upon bison numerous as ants, pronghorn antelope like floods of tawny salmon, elk swarming like bees. At times I would turn my head to the side and gulp for air like a swimmer who can't keep her face in the water one second longer. It was as if the sight was too much to be inhaled in one breath or a thousand breaths.

Suddenly emotion surged up in my throat and a thought flooded my consciousness. *Can you feel their love?* What a strange question! It came uninvited, and I puzzled over it only a moment before tossing it aside. Then another thought: *In your life, you can have many homes all at once.* I pushed this one away, too, and slid from my rock, agitated by something, nothing. Arrow abandoned the stick she had been trying unsuccessfully to yank from the snow and hurried ahead of me.

We walked on and on. A sudden snowfall dropped flakes as big and fluffy as marshmallows. Snow does not fall silently. If you listen closely, you can hear it coming to earth with a soft, confiding sound, something between a whisper and a hiss. When I passed a few old posts and a cattle guard and headed into a wide pasture, Arrow dropped back and began following silently behind me. I walked on without taking notice of the fact that she was falling farther and farther behind.

Arrow whined nervously. Turning, I saw that she had returned to sit at the cattle guard. When I called to her, she came to me only to nudge my arm and run back toward the fence posts. Arrow is never one to call off a walk, so I collected my thoughts and looked around. I couldn't recall when the snow had stopped falling. Tall canyon walls loomed around us, somehow threatening. The sky lowered above our heads, its luminescent, yellow-gray color eerie, jaundiced. Arrow woofed softly and headed back the way we had come. Unhesitatingly, I followed. I don't know what she sensed—a bear, a puma, a person? It could have been any of those things, or nothing.

Perhaps she hurried me back down the trail because she knew what I was to see there, and her timing had to be perfect.

We had walked for maybe a mile when I was startled by a crashing noise on the hillside to my right. The sound was like snow breaking off in a huge clump and whooshing downhill. Out of the corner of my eye, I first saw it: a desperate chase. A chase like I'd never seen. An enormous doe was leaping through the sagebrush above me. At her flanks in the deep snow ran a lunging coyote, mouth open, red tongue flapping. Arrow

stopped and pushed back against me, just in time. The trail the
deer was carving sent her hurtling onto our path, almost within
arm's reach. I could feel the labor of her breath as she sprang
past me. Snow sprayed down on us for an instant and I heard
hooves slap on the packed snow of the road. Then she was over
the far bank, springing her way into an open meadow.

Now the coyote leaped onto the path—and froze. For a
long moment, he held our eyes. Arrow whined and leaned
toward him. He stepped toward us and paused, confused. Then
he stepped toward the deer, now lunging through belly-deep
snow in the meadow. The coyote glanced at Arrow, then me,
then the deer. On snow-crusted feet, he turned and trotted back
up the hill and into the sagebrush. I watched his plume of a tail
until he vanished into the undergrowth like vapor. The deer was
at the edge of the woods, still running. Standing rock-still, I
took great gulps of air, as though I too had raced across the
frozen hillside.

At the car, I rummaged through my luggage to find my
totem guidebooks. In *Animalspeak*, I looked up "coyote": "Coyotes keep a den for years, but don't live there all the time." *Home,
homesickness.* "Coyotes may teach the value of having a base that
you move out from." *You will have many homes, all at once.* My daydream at the stream returned to me. The thoughts I had thrown
away, I searched for and found again. *Did you feel their love?* The
animals in Yellowstone. My loneliness for them. I looked up
deer: "Deer expresses a gentle love that can open new doors."

Over my head, I heard a call, like the soft tinkling of tiny bells. It was an osprey, circling high above the car. "Hawk medicine teaches you to be observant. Life is sending you signals and messages."

And the Bull Uttered One Word

by Joanne Elizabeth Lauck

"Grief is the binding alloy of the armoring about the heart. Like a fire touched, the mind recoils at losing what it holds most dear. As the mind contracts about its grief, the spaciousness of the heart often seems very distant."

—STEPHEN LEVINE

My dog Leaf died on a Wednesday afternoon. I held him as the veterinarian administered the lethal injection, the smell of his fur imprinting itself on my memory. Already in a deep sleep from a mild tranquilizer, he never stirred. Although many believe that losing a pet and losing a human family member or close friend are two different experiences, I found that the pain of loss and the process of grieving crossed those boundaries as readily as the love had.

I had what the experts on pet loss and human bereavement call an uncommon relationship with Leaf. Our natural affinity, a bonding of the most spacious heartfelt kind, was in truth a relationship of extraordinary depth and scope. In dreaming and in waking, Leaf, as ally and elder, had played a central role in my self explorations, linking me to the teaching of his wild ancestors and helping me navigate the complexities of human relationships for over thirteen years.

I thought I had released him, willing to be taught and transformed by this final experience. But the day he died I staggered under the weight of the loss. The surety that had accompanied me up to that moment fled to some dark burrow of my mind. I faced the reality of his death, uncomforted. I must have walked the neighborhood for hours, trying to escape the gut-wrenching feelings that pinched my insides like a vise. I finally returned home with a tenuous calm borne from exhaustion.

Death closes familiar doors. Stephen Levine, a pioneer in the investigation of conscious living and dying, notes that in the first phase of grief, you experience how the now-absent loved one acted as a mirror, reflecting back that place inside yourself that is love. And it is the loss of the connection to that aspect of self that brings such acute pain.

Some vital inner circuitry felt severed the moment Leaf died. The pain stunned me. That night I looked forward to sleep, seeking relief and hoping for a dream. For years I had pursued the night's dream images with great anticipation, and Leaf's death merely amplified those feelings. I knew that dream images were an integral part of any growth or healing process and that they might provide focus and information in my struggle to rebuild a life without him.

The next morning I returned from the night's dreaming with only a single phrase:

"The bull uttered one word."

While incomprehensible to anyone else, I recognized the phrase immediately. It occurred in a powerful initiatory dream years ago in which I was lured out of my house by an animal ally. I found myself in a field where a cow charged me. Twice I retreated, narrowly escaping her lowered horns and the force of her body. But the third time a fence at my back prevented my escape. At the moment of impact, when I knew I would die, a bull witnessing the charge uttered one word. I died, shattering into a million pieces that were instantly whisked away.

I understood, even at that time in my studies, that images of death and dismemberment signaled a new beginning. Dreams always mark the normal growth process, sending timeless initiatory symbols when energies are released and old ways of thinking and acting are broken.

In shamanistic traditions worldwide, animals typically act as initiators, the vehicles of the deaths that destroy the known self and permit change. Both cow and bull were animals associated with the womb and regeneration and once played a rich and complex role in ancient religions. The dream had initiated me into an ancient shamanistic world, heralding a new cycle of dreaming populated with animals.

In the wake of Leaf's death, the one phrase brought the dream back into my awareness. I read through my old journal notes. They contained more questions than answers. The cow was charging me. Was she recharging me? I had looked up the word *charge*. It meant to impose a task or responsibility on, or to load, or fill to capacity.

I was certain, looking back, that the task imposed at the time of the initial dream was to consciously open to the new direction unfolding in my waking and dreaming life. The cow had charged me, shattering my boundaries and whisking me into a new zone of experience. And I could only guess that the word the bull uttered was akin to the biblical word from which new creation sprang into being.

But what did it mean now? I mulled over the images of this old dream and their emergence into my present field of "charged" events. A new world had of necessity sprung into being with Leaf's absence. Part of that new world focused on my need to fully understand our relationship and give voice to it, a need largely unformed until I felt his imminent death and anticipated living without him. I didn't press the dream interpretation further, not wanting to restrict its multilayered message. I knew in time I would understand more.

The next day I picked up Leaf's ashes. Hardened against

the pain, I felt only anger, unmoved by reason or recent insight. I went to bed early and fell into a fitful sleep. I dreamed:

> I was trying to find food. On the sidewalk ahead was a small black dog, injured and bleeding. I knew I couldn't just leave him, so I picked him up and began searching for a veterinarian.

Like the dream phrase from the previous night, the image of the little dog took me back in time. I returned to the memory of an incident four years earlier when I witnessed the violent death of a little black dog. I was driving on a major street during rush-hour traffic. I saw a small dog on the curb. Still several cars away, I watched as he left the safety of the curb and entered the street. He was hit. Horrified, I watched as he got up, crippled by the blow, and took a few more steps. He was hit again and still again, until his crumpled form was thrown to the far side of the road. I swung the car around, parking haphazardly, and reached him just in time to witness the last breath leaving his small battered form.

As I gathered his broken body in my arms, tears streamed down my face. I cried intermittently throughout the day, the scene replaying itself in my mind with brutal clarity. The fact that I hadn't known the dog didn't seem to matter. I had witnessed his apparently futile and brutal death without being able to intervene, and had been touched in some deep way.

I spent days struggling to understand the experience. I believed then, as I do now, that pattern and purpose direct all encounters, but his death hadn't made sense. I combed the area for the dog's owner. No one had seen him before. It was as though he had appeared out of thin air.

I remember picking up Kahlil Gibran's *The Prophet* and reading, "Your pain is the breaking of the shell of your understanding." An idea hammered away at me. Was I being asked to address my fear of death and penetrate its dark mystery? I had read that those wise in shamanic traditions considered death an adviser. How would I live if I were open to death's teachings?

I never forgot the experience. Some months later I relived the little dog's death in a dream. The details in the dream were identical to the actual experience except at the end I lifted the small broken body up in the air in a gesture of supplication, asking God "to take care of this little one."

"You always have to break every bone in your body," advised my brother in still another dream, two weeks before Leaf died. Being broken, dying, is necessary, essential, for new life. Can we lift our broken selves up in compassionate surrender? Can we trust the pain as well as the light and let ourselves be reshaped by its harsh touch?

I endured Leaf's absence, the wounded part of me struggling to deepen my trust and acceptance of his death, as years ago, I had struggled with the little black dog's death. And now the little dog had returned in a dream, injured and bleeding in the middle of my path.

Psychologist James Hillman, who has collected dreams with animals in them since 1960, says that animals enter our lives in waking or dreaming because they have wisdom to impart. Animals in dreams reflect soul energies. They come to help us see when we are in darkness.

Primitive societies believed each person had a bush soul and a human soul. The bush soul incarnates as an animal or tree with which the person has an affinity or psychic connection. And when the bush soul is injured, the person is considered injured as well.

As a carrier of soul energies or bush soul image, the little black dog's injuries in the current dream mirrored my own, his broken bones, my own broken structure. As I sought food, perhaps sustenance for a broken heart, his dream presence in front of me reminded me of the sacrifice necessary for growth, redirecting me toward the inner animal doctor, the source of instinctual wisdom.

Consider the possibility that each one of us sees the images we need to see and hears the voices we need to hear to initiate our own rite of passage, our own healing and growth. We can dream those images. Or we can draw from the natural world the physical presence that will fit the unique contours of our psyches. Perhaps the soul listens intently for the sounds and images that will resonate within us, and then brings them to us.

They in turn, propelled by voices we shall never hear, carry us from the pain of the fearful, clinging mind to the spaciousness of the heart, activating the healing energies of our most fundamental self.

In her autobiography *Home to the Wilderness* (Penguin 1974), nature writer Sally Carrighar shares a moving account of this innate ability to draw to ourselves the particular animal presence with the potential to reconnect our known self with its deepest intent and wisdom. Her animal presence was a much-loved small white dog whom she was forced to abandon when she was a child. Years later, after a number of setbacks, Carrighar decided to end her life. She took a handful of sleeping pills, and then, as she prepared to swallow the rest, she heard a dog bark:

> I was startled, for it seemed the bark of the little white dog I had betrayed long ago. He kept on barking, and I thought of the way he had tried to keep up with my bicycle going down the hill, of my last glimpse of his flying feet and the wind flinging back his ears. Was it indeed the same dog, sending a message across the years, a needed hallucination—or an actual dog … that night? If an actual living dog, how did I know he was white? Perhaps fate was reaching me with the only voice to which I could respond.

She threw the rest of the pills out the window and fell into a deep sleep. Waking or dreaming, psychic or actual event, some presence reached her as my little black dog reached me, bridging both waking and dreaming realities with inexplicable ease.

As the month after Leaf's death slowly passed, I felt a subtle resistance perpetuated by the angry and wounded part of myself that only wanted Leaf back. It was impeding the movement of healing forces through me. Outer events intruded. A great weariness enveloped me. I resented the growing hub of activity that displaced my time alone to grieve, as well as the family's return to a normalcy I didn't feel. As I held on to my wounded stance, absorbed in my grief, I had another dream that prodded me from this narrow ledge of resistance.

> I was walking by a house when a small white dog, growling viciously, charged out of the house at me. Before I could raise my hand in defense, the dog leaped up and bit me on the cheek, holding the length of its body in such a way that it pinned my left arm underneath it. I couldn't get the dog off. Its sharp teeth were embedded firmly in my cheek, its body a straitjacket preventing all movement of my left arm and hand. I called loudly for help. Finally a neighbor removed the dog, and I began to sob as I remembered that Leaf was gone.

I woke up crying. As the tears subsided, I recorded the dream, acutely aware that being detained or questioned, bitten or pursued by an animal, in waking or dreaming, means the animal has something to tell you. Why did this dog bite me and then hang on? Was I hanging on? The dog's body blocked my left side—the side depth psychology associates with the intuitive faculty, the feminine, and the unconscious link with the mysterious depths of primeval intelligence and pattern. Was I blocking this channel? The question landed inside me. With a familiar click of recognition, the meaning slid into place. My resentment of life's forward thrust, my reluctance to let go of Leaf's physical presence in my life, both products of the separating mind, were indeed blocking this inner channel. Preserving my wounded self impeded a natural source of guidance from my unconscious and prevented me from accessing my heart.

"Let there be no purpose in friendship save the deepening of the spirit," said Gibran's Prophet. "For love that seeks aught but the disclosure of its own mystery is not love but a net cast forth: and only the unprofitable is caught."

I let go of my wounded stance, let go of holding on to the relationship in its familiar form, and in the midst of my loss, in the midst of my protest, everything felt hallowed with meaning.

My energy and spirit returned. Several weeks later, as though in joyful confirmation of my new understanding, Leaf came to me in the dream state, not as an animal familiar, but as the being who had shared my waking life with me.

I had been immersed in some now-forgotten dream sequence when suddenly he was there at the edge of the dream's activity. He sat quietly, his warm brown eyes staring at me intensely. I stopped whatever I had been doing in the dream, my eyes drawn into the depths of his loving gaze. We looked at each other across time and space, connected beyond words in heartfelt union. I knew that he had to remain at the intersection between our worlds. With a solemn and sweet expression, he assured me, in that silent language of the heart, that he should be there, supporting and loving me while I continued my life and the work I had come to do. I awoke feeling his presence at the edge of my awareness, feeling the imprint of his gaze.

This was to be his only visit that year. But it was enough. I had crossed the bridge. I had traveled beyond the armoring, the self-doubts, the judgments, to enter the spaciousness of the heart where there was only one of us. In the months that followed, the ebb and flow of emotions continued, frequently overshadowing my recent understanding, as the process of letting go worked its way through me. But never again was I so drastically separated from the grace of our abiding connection.

Stephen Levine reminds us that "the toll for crossing to the other shore of wholeness is the relinquishment of our suffering. This crossing over is what is called healing; it costs each of us identification with 'my pain.' It may even mean that our lives will never be the same."

And the bull uttered one word.

POSTSCRIPT: The little black dog appeared again in a dream while I was writing this story. I dreamed:

> I am in a class. Eight of us sit on the floor in a circle. The facilitator appears to be a yoga instructor. He wants us to take turns speaking about when we were last pushed to grow beyond our ideas and self-images. When it is my turn to share, I sit in concentrated silence, trying to formulate my thoughts on the subject. After an indeterminable length of time, the instructor gets up and runs out the patio door and into a field. I watch him leave, and then before my astonished eyes, he changes into the little black dog. The dog waits in the field for me. I race out to him and throw my arms around him, crying tears of joy. As I stroke him in happy comprehension, my classmates stand next to us, beaming.

Woman and Wolf

By Cynthia Clay

On Christmas Eve, I was in the hospital for a skin graft. The outside of my left calf had received second- and third-degree burns from a heating pad. Because of my diabetes and resultant nerve damage, I did not feel the burn when it occurred. My right

leg had been amputated ten years before because of a paper
staple puncture. The diabetes and immune-suppressant drugs
for a kidney transplant I'd had the year before made healing a
slow process for me.

So there I was again in a hospital bed, filled with fear, guilt,
hope, disgust, anxiety. Although my precious service dog,
Napoleon, a seventy-five-pound black Lab, resided in my
hospital room on a special "made-just-for-him" bed, it was not
enough. I needed more. I have a spirit guide/angel named
Mirium who helps me in times of great challenge. I became
aware of her presence right after the amputation of my leg ten
years earlier. I am well aware she may be, and probably is, a projection of my higher self. No matter—whatever works. Her
presence always brings me comfort, be it through peace of mind
or gentle humor. Seldom is she wrong about the future or things
I should pursue.

From the first day of the skin graft surgery, Mirium was
calmly angry and negative about the graft. This disturbed me,
as the skin graft process would shorten my healing time from
about ten months to one. I wanted the graft to work so I could
resume my very active life of counseling, public speaking, training, and other anticipated adventures.

The morning of Christmas Eve, I read the story in *Animals
as Teachers and Healers* about Waluna the wolf, who with play-
nips and gentle licks to a large scar on a woman's face began that
woman's emotional healing. Animals have always been near me

to help me through difficult emotional times, but what about physical healing? What about this skin graft? I decided to ask the spirit of Waluna to help me heal. I actually visualized Waluna gently lying against my wound as her icy blue eyes stared into my desperate blue ones.

During that day, I began to feel a powerful yet playful melding and bonding between Mirium and Waluna. Mirium's anger and negativity were dissipating as Waluna's presence became stronger. By that evening I was actually resting and even sleeping in a calm quiet of hope.

The next morning was Christmas Day. The tension in my room was high. The morning began with doctors in scrubs and masks milling around my bed. Nurses and burn unit technicians hurried in and out with wound care equipment. As the unveiling began, all eyes widened. The fragile graft had taken! I knew that with my medical history the odds had been stacked heavily against me. One doctor came in, looked at the graft, then looked at me. We both gave the graft a thumbs-up and a *"Yes!"* I began to cry. The doctor came to the side of my bed and took my hand. He said, "No one else thought you could do this. I knew you could. The feisty ones always heal better."

At that very moment I realized the source of Mirium's anger and negativity. She had been angry with the medical team and its pessimism about my healing. I also realized Mirium welcomed the powerful presence of Waluna and the protection Waluna gave my wound. In my mind's eye, between the tears, I thanked Mirium and Waluna. I saw Waluna sitting, with Mirium kneeling on one knee next to her. In that visualization, I imagined that Mirium was showing me how she appreciated my calling to Waluna's spirit. Mirium now had an animal companion of her own, just as I had my Napoleon.

CHAPTER SIX

Grief, Guilt, and Atonement

"Our animals shepherd us through certain eras of our lives. When we are ready to turn the corner and make it on our own . . . they let us go."

—ANONYMOUS

In my first book, a chapter called "Going Gently" focused on healing and insights that animals can bring to their human companions regarding death and dying. This chapter was twice as long as any of the others because the majority of the mail I received spoke to this aspect of the human-animal relationship.

Since writing that chapter, I realize that there is a particular world of experience I did not address concerning death and dying. These are the stories that didn't end well, stories of inner wounds that became infected with guilt and shame and are achingly slow to heal, if indeed they heal at all. "The tears I cried last night were not only for the stories in your book, but for my own untold stories about animals—the ones in which they did not fare well," wrote one reader. "We need to hear those stories, the ones that have not been told."

I have a file in my desk thick with stories that have not been told. Stories of guilt, grief, and remorse about the animals in our care. Often after a lecture or reading, several people will approach me with stories that end with "I should have known...I should have been there...I can't forgive myself...I can't forget." In fact, no one issue comes to the forefront more frequently than people lamenting over guilt: over unnoticed illness, accidents, dangers not recognized, communications not understood; careless acts committed out of naïveté, simple oversight, or ignorance. Even over circumstances clearly beyond human control. The "if only" of guilt became a symphony of pain, despair, self-recriminations, and whys that I heard at every speaking engagement I gave. Time and again, I would listen to these stories and try to offer some kind of heartfelt solace. Repeatedly I would ask myself, "What does it take to reconcile ourselves to such painful losses? How do we move beyond the heartbreak of a loss for which we feel at fault in some way?"

Many people admitted that the grief they felt at the death of their pets was beyond any pain they had experienced in their entire lives. They also admitted that with the ache of that loss came a great burden of guilt and responsibility. These tragic experiences sometimes involve a drama of hideous coincidences, but more often are simply a subtle unfolding of sad events. Although the incidents differ one from another, the shame and blame that fuel them sound remarkably similar:

Years ago, my life was in emotional and financial upheaval, and my sole support was a German shepherd puppy named Tacky. The people I was staying with weren't allowed to keep pets, so I left Tacky in the care of a friend who lived on a big lake with her collie named Rowdy. Then I returned home and began looking for a job.

A week later, my friend called to tell me that Tacky had drowned at a nearby mill on the lake. Peeled bark floating on the mill pond looked dry and solid. Fishermen often tossed their bait or fish trimmings into the pond. Tacky and Rowdy apparently tried to walk onto the bark to get these tasty morsels and fell through. They couldn't climb back up onto the bark or get past it to the safety of the bank. My friend heard Rowdy barking and managed to get to the lake and pull him out, but it was too late for Tacky.

When I heard the news, I collapsed and sobbed for the next twenty hours. My friends were afraid I would have to be hospitalized. My thoughts returned again and again to Tacky. She couldn't have understood why I'd left her, why I did not come when she needed me. When my body finally and totally betrayed me and her by running out of tears, and by going on breathing and pumping blood when she lay cold and alone, I was stunned to have survived so much pain. I thought, I will now be able to go on living when my mother dies.

—SYN FERGUSON

I decided not to wait until my chow, Rachel, was incapacitated by her cancer, which, I was told, would soon eat through her bone and affect her vision and brain. She was put to sleep just three months after her fifth birthday. Even though I made the decision not to wait until the last minute, there is the constant doubt: what if the doctors were wrong? What if she could have gotten better with time? What did I *not* do? I still cry myself to sleep.

—ANNETTE HAGGARD

I lost my beloved cat Sir Lancelot on Valentine's Day due to kidney failure. It all happened so fast I still can't believe he is gone. Over the last three to four months, he'd become aggressive and the vet said that it was possible he had a brain tumor. The vet said there was no way I could have possibly known, but still I feel guilty.

—DEBI REIMANN

In my own life, I have had many experiences with animals and death in which I felt shame and guilt. My animal companions at Brightstar Farm continue to bring me even more painful grist for the mill. After four and a half decades of guilt-ridden partings, I have come to believe that my especially painful situations with animals have little to do with the animals and everything to do with myself and my human frailties, fears, and unhealed emotional wounds. Most stuff I clutch tight to my chest about animals isn't really about animals at all. I believe that animals bless me with experiences, sometimes at the cost of their own lives, that churn up my buried apprehensions and help me face what I need to face. Animals provide an opportunity for me to look at my issues. And because I, like so many people, have such deep-seated fears and confusion surrounding death, many of my most disturbing and profound experiences with animals are centered around this topic.

If a difficult issue arises in a human and animal partnership, most likely the issue belongs to the human. At a workshop, a woman told a story of the death of her cat. In the cat's last hours, the woman phoned her estranged husband. At the time they were embroiled in a grim divorce, but she knew how much the cat meant to her embittered mate. She explained to the workshop participants, "Nothing but that cat could have made me speak to my husband in a civil tone, but I called because I couldn't let Sissy die without his knowledge. He had loved her so much."

Another woman talked about her deaf dog, who is difficult to live with. She admits that her greatest challenge is learning to truly listen to people.

A woman came up to me after a book reading and told me about being raped many years earlier. She survived emotionally by getting a large dog with a big heart and a goofy grin, who became her protector and "soul mate." When this dog died years later, the woman was completely beside herself with grief and was hospitalized for a time. Yet she admitted that she quickly recognized her grief was only in part because of the passing of her beloved friend. "I was grieving the rape, the memories, and the fears that I now had to face because my wonderful protector was gone." In all these cases, the real challenges belonged not to the animals, but to their human companions.

These traumatic and unsettling experiences with animals I call sticky business or the sticky stuff. Such memories just seem to stick to us until we have acknowledged their many-layered impact upon our lives. I can talk about the experience, write about it, and ponder it, and still it might stick in my throat until all of the learning, forgiving, and mending is complete. The process can take months or even years, depending on my willingness to embrace the grief and remorse, which sometimes seem blinding in their intensity. When I have looked at the experience from every possible direction and extracted whatever messages it brings to my life, my throat clears and my mouth finally tastes clean again. Afterwards, I usually find myself better for the pain, burned clean and fresh and wiser for all my self-recrimination and self-blame.

In his helpful book *The Loss of a Pet*, Wallace Sife, M.D., tackles the unsettling topic of guilt. He defines guilt as our normal response to some failed duty or obligation we feel we were competent to perform, and points out that guilt is a common aspect of normal bereavement. In fact, it is unlikely that we won't feel some stab of guilt over things not said, not done, or not understood during the course of our mourning.

In our relationship with an animal companion, Sife explains, we customarily take upon ourselves total and complete responsibility concerning every aspect of that animal's life, including food and water, medical treatment, playmates, sexuality, and quality of life. So powerful is our control over the life and fate of an animal companion that we sometimes become unconsciously convinced that our control exceeds even the power of death. Because we care for our animal companion so deeply, we may secretly come to believe that we can control this fearsome aspect of a dying animal's life through the sheer strength of our affection. Of course we can't. When an animal companion dies, says Sife, "the shock easily can be distorted into an intensified sense of personal inadequacy and guilt. In effect, our emotions tell us we have failed in some way to perform as well as we should have. It makes us feel as if we are responsible for letting the pet die."

Enid Traisman, M.S.W., who is a grief counselor for the

Dove Lewis Pet Loss and Bereavement program in Portland, Oregon, supports Sife's insights. "So many people are plagued by guilt at the loss of a pet. They express guilt over many things: speaking harshly when the pet had a potty accident, choosing euthanasia too late or too soon, not getting a second medical opinion. Some regret letting the pet go outside into a danger zone, others regret never letting their pets outside often enough. Guilt, which is anger turned inward, is a normal response in the grieving process—the first basic feeling once a person has moved through shock." Enid continues: "Most people can work through this guilt or anger by going over the chain of events that lead to an animal's death, and accepting that they did the best they could *at that moment in time.* No hindsight is allowed here! It will only lead to 'if only.'"

Human partners can assume a godlike role in an animal's life, leading to lessons in fallibility. Psychologist Kim Rosen, who pioneered human-dolphin swims as a form of psychotherapy, suggests that when we feel a near-desperate need to exert control over death, we may be confronting our "inability to accept the simple and very real condition of human helplessness."

Quite honestly, I cringe at the word *helpless.* For me, admitting my helplessness in certain situations signifies loss of control. Somehow I feel that if I can retain some fantasy of control by assigning fault to myself and playing "if only" tapes over and over in my mind, I will not have to face the fact that there have been and will be many times in my life when I am simply and utterly helpless.

When my first dog, Keesha, was overtaken with cancer, I clutched at every opportunity I could to lay blame and fault. That was, of course, after I tried desperately to deny that she had cancer to begin with. "The veterinarian made too hasty a diagnosis," I told myself. So I took her to two other vets, who shook their heads sadly and gave me the same bad news. Next I tried to believe the biopsy was wrong.

Eventually there were weeks of radiation treatments that did not help. And I told myself that *if only* the radiation lab had done a better job, Keesha would be healing. When my dog came home from the vet hospital to die, I turned my need for control upon myself. *If only* I had found the tumor earlier. *If only* I could afford different, better, experimental treatment. *If only* I had known that the medication I gave her to control her flea allergies was so debilitating. *If only* I could pinpoint the mistakes—because surely this cancer was all just a terrible mistake—then maybe the next time I could prevail over death.

It took years of gentleness with myself to put aside my guilt and anger at Keesha's death. Even today, I am assailed by losses I find hard to reconcile, but I am learning to accept a certain measure of helplessness, because in truth, the only way to avoid the death of an animal companion is to choose to have no animal family at all.

A woman who had lost her dog after its long, debilitating illness spoke to me about her terrible guilt at euthanizing her dog "perhaps a day or so too early." Before her dog died, she spent months carrying the dog with her wherever she went because the dog couldn't move. She stayed awake nights for her dog and even quit her job to care for him. In the end, she beat herself up emotionally because she had perhaps missed a precious twenty-four or forty-eight more hours with her dying friend. When I asked her to consider all the months her tremendous devotion had brought to them both, months her veterinarian considered a medical miracle, she could focus only on the two days he might have had and on the actual euthanasia process, which didn't go smoothly. She had been carrying this guilt around with her for years and showed no willingness to put it down. I cannot help but believe that such self-blame is a way to avoid the fact that we are often helpless. Death includes far more than the details we become fixated upon. It includes moments of frailty and lack of control, but it also offers a much larger tapestry of a life lived, of moments of joy and enchantment and companionship—and often magnificent courage on the part of the animal and its human companion during those last days of life.

When grief paralyzes us this completely, I believe that professional counseling can be beneficial. When we discover why we are so determined to live in such pain, we are on the path to real healing. Finding the way out of this maze is the gift of counseling. For those embarrassed to seek professional help in dealing with the loss of a pet, I tell them that they owe this to the memory of their beloved animal companion. Furthermore, our animal companions would never wish such misery upon us. We do not honor the dead by suffering. Rather, our determined efforts to heal speak most honorably to the legacy of love and devotion our animals left us.

It is difficult to have our omnipotency challenged when an animal companion dies despite all our good care and love, but to have a precious companion die because of neglect or careless-ness is as close to mortal agony as some of us will ever come. An old fence collapses and our wandering horse is struck by a car. A gate is left open and our dog never returns home again. Poisonous antifreeze drips onto a garage floor and we watch helplessly as our cat dies in agony. We back the car out and acci-dentally crush an animal companion who was napping beneath the rear wheel. "I killed him . . . I poisoned her," we say in raging despair and shame. Perhaps we are ultimately responsible in such cases. And yet we must somehow learn to accept that no human being can be ever-vigilant in each moment of life. Acci-dents do happen to all of us. Rationally I know this, but shame and guilt hide in hearts, not in minds. And my heart knows this all too well.

At Brightstar Farm, I have a flock of chickens that I call my chicken family. I adore them. Although my chickens run free during the day and forage in our yard as well as in the neighbors' pastures, at night I keep them in a small, dilapidated henhouse for their protection. Putting the chickens to bed is an evening ritual I cherish. As the chickens cluck on their perches above me, I gather eggs from the hay-filled nest boxes. As I put the eggs in my pocket, I thank the chickens and bid them good night. Then I lock the two latches on the door and close off the other entry hole in back of the henhouse. If I don't take these precautions, Ever Vigilant the raccoon comes visiting. He considers the henhouse and its inhabitants his personal smorgasbord and never misses an opportunity to dine. I know this because I have had house sitters forget to lock up, and the results are always bloody and heartbreaking. Whenever this happened, it was easy to blame the house sitters for the deaths. My anger at them helped ease the pain of losing a treasured member of the flock.

One spring night, a favorite hen of mine, a fuzzy black silkie banty, hatched out her first-of-the-season clutch of eight fat eggs. The chicks were exquisite, about the size of a walnut and each a soft shade of gray, yellow, buff, or red. I fashioned a special wire pen for them and their doting mother inside the henhouse so that they could get their feet beneath them before taking on the big world of the outside yard. Before I closed up the henhouse that night, I spent extra time cuddling the chicks. As I lifted each chick, I complimented the silkie on her beautiful brood; she clucked in pride and gazed into my face, nodding her head right and left. Mesmerized by my new chicken family, I walked out of the henhouse in a fog of goodwill. The stars were bright beneath a chromium moon. In my pocket were a handful of brown and white eggs. I never gave a second thought to the latch on the henhouse door.

In the middle of the night, I heard Arrow growl at the back door and utter a stream of worried barks. I called out to her to be quiet and pulled the covers up over my head.

The following morning, I walked into the backyard and immediately noticed a trail of feathers from the henhouse door. The feathers led to a bundle of blood, bone, and flesh discarded on our gravel driveway—all that remained of our largest red laying hen. "No, no . . . oh, God, no," I groaned while I hurried toward the sounds of confusion behind the henhouse door. Arrow raced across the yard barking wildly, tail up and shoulder hackles erect like spikes. Her nose followed the path of the intruder across the driveway, over the porch, beneath the fence, and away. When I pulled aside the door, my stomach lurched. On the dirt floor lay the shredded body of our small red mil-fleure hen, Henrietta. Three years before, she had been one of the first banty chicks we had brought home to Brightstar Farm and raised in our kitchen. Surrounding Henrietta was a scattering of what looked like small, colored stones. My eyes flew to the silkie in her makeshift pen. She paced frantically along the chicken wire, calling out for her babies, her eyes wide and frightened. One lone chick fluttered along behind her, its peep ceaseless, like an alarm beeper. I squeezed my eyes shut in horror: The stones were the remains of the silkie chicks, torn one by one from their chicken-wire pen, then tossed aside. I don't know how long I stood there and took in the hideous scene. This time, there was no balm of anger and blame to heap on anyone but myself. And the anger I poured on myself felt hot and vile. My heart ached. My shoulders slumped. I shrank in my guilt and grief.

Every day our chickens wander the yard, facing the coyotes, the hawks, and the neighborhood dogs with their own wit and caution. Because they are free-range chickens, their safety rests on their own feathered shoulders, and I have accepted with sadness the occasional death of a chicken as part of my choice to let them run free. But at night, when they come home to roost, their welfare rests on my shoulders. With a few locks and some attentiveness, I can assure them of a safe haven for the night. In my heart, I imagined that they had depended on that. And I told myself that I had failed them completely.

The following evening, a rare experience with my old aracana hen fueled my guilt to new heights. When I counted the chickens in the henhouse that night, I noticed her absence. Perhaps she decided to take her chances elsewhere, I told myself, since thanks to me the henhouse was clearly no safe house. I looked for her in the barn, in the garage, in all of her old roosts, and found her nowhere. In the dark, I gave up my hunt and headed for the house. As I approached our back porch, I noticed a large brown blob against the back door. Sure enough, it was the aracana. Last winter I had treated her for injuries in a battle with a coyote. Each day, sitting on the porch near the back door, I had soaked her behind in a bucket of warm water and rubbed ointment into her wounds. She never protested. The instant I saw her there at the door, I realized that she was taking refuge in the only safe place she remembered—the porch where she had been cared for.

The old hen clucked softly when I picked her up and carried her to the henhouse. "I'm so very, very sorry," I murmured into her feathers. "I'll try to protect you better. I promise that the henhouse will be a safer place. Sometimes I make terrible mistakes. Forgive me." I placed her high up onto a roost. For the next three nights, she appeared at the back door, a painful reminder. Finally she returned to the henhouse on her own.

The chicken disaster was especially traumatic because of the high cost of my negligence. I *could* have made a difference. Even so, regret and self-condemnation would not bring back the silkie's chicks or keep the henhouse safe in the future. As a result of that experience, I have created my own tools to deal with my failings. First, I remind myself that in this and all other instances, *I am not perfect*. The chickens taught me a lesson about my hopeless quest for perfection. That no one is perfect is something I hate to acknowledge. Because if I can believe in perfection, I will have another reason to believe in my power to control. I tell myself, "If I had done it right with the chickens, I could have ensured life and peace. If I can always do it right and perfect, my control over fate will be so much stronger..." or so I delude myself.

I read about a man's beloved poodle who was snatched up by an alligator as they walked along a Florida golf course together. The gator appeared out of nowhere, grabbed the dog, and swiftly pulled it under the water while the owner watched in horror. I hope that man is not as obsessed with perfection as I am, because in a perfect world, alligators don't prey on little dogs on a golf course, and women don't forget to latch chicken houses. Perfection is a destructive illusion. I bless my chickens for making me more aware. This experience reminds me to keep looking at my issues with helplessness, guilt, control, and perfection no matter how much I want to push away such thoughts.

DECIDING WHETHER AND WHEN to euthanize an animal companion carries a unique burden of guilt. I have had to euthanize some of my animal friends, and I understood fully at the instant of their death that I was ending their lives. It felt as if I were killing them. This is the burden I face at euthanasia: how to reconcile myself to ending the very life of an animal I dearly love. Euthanasia can feel as though we are cutting off a part of our heart and spirit.

Although I believe it is ideal to let an animal companion die a natural death, sometimes such a death becomes too painful or prolonged to endure for both the animal itself and those of us sitting in vigil. Sometimes keeping an old or ailing animal alive will utterly drain a family's financial, physical, and emotional resources. So we make the painful decision to euthanize the animal and then discover we despise ourselves for what we perceive as our selfishness.

That is exactly how I felt after euthanizing my wonderful young cat Bear, who suffered from an unending sequence of urinary tract infections. I could not imagine letting him continue to suffer and die screaming in pain, so I made the decision to have him euthanized. After he was dead, I could not help feeling relief. Our household relaxed, our vet bills plummeted, and the terrible crying and pacing of a twenty-pound orange furball in chronic pain ceased. I even noticed how much extra housecleaning Bear's long-haired coat had created for me—another unexpected "bonus" of his passing. For this momentary relief, I beat myself up emotionally for many months. I asked myself, "How could I kill the cat who had loved me beyond anything in his life, and then be despicable enough to feel a sense of relief about it? What sort of monster was I?" For months after his death, I wept daily and my self-esteem shrank to nothing. Three years after Bear's death, I still feel a vague sense of guilt.

To address this guilt, I have turned to many useful psychological and spiritual tools that I will elaborate upon in this chapter. Each brought me a measure of peace. Today I realize that Bear has become one of my most profound teachers. He is my litmus test. Whenever I speak to people about letting go of guilt and grief and moving on, I am forced to consider how far I have progressed in letting go of Bear. His death reminds me of how deep these hurts go. When I pass Bear's grave by the willow tree these days, I am inclined to honor the deep bond I have with him rather than judge myself yet another time over the circumstances of his death. He has given me a gift of insight that empowers me when I help others navigate the dark waters of a pet's euthanasia.

Many people carry guilt and regret over actions they committed years ago when they held different values, or even when they were children. Roger Fuchs shared a story with me about his adolescent days as a trapper. As a young man, he would set out a line of steel-jawed traps and sell animal hides for extra pocket money. One day he found a mink in one of his traps. Trying to offer her a quick and painfree death, he inadvertently let a trap close around her neck and head. The memory of her shrieks of agony still ring in his ears thirty years later. Today the traps gather dust in a box in his garage, and whenever he sees them, he winces. "I didn't know differently then," he admitted. "All those lives I took and never understood what suffering I was causing."

My first husband was also a trapper in his youth. He quit the day he found a young male bobcat in one of his traps. A storm had prevented him from checking his trapline each day, and by the time he found the bobcat a week later in a shallow cave, it was gaunt, fevered, and close to death. Across its front paw, the leg-hold trap bit deep into gangrenous flesh. He told me that the bobcat looked at him with eyes wet and vacant with sickness. He shot the animal and never set another trap. "How could I take a life when I had no power to give life? What was I thinking?"

When I was about eight years old, I would act out the power-lessness I felt as a child against our first dog, a gentle black German shepherd named Lady. On our daily walks together, I would hit her when she disobeyed me and my stern commands. To this day, I remember her cringing once and crying out when I struck her across the back with the end of her leash, once, twice, three times. Now in my forties, I can honestly say that no memory in my entire life brings me more anguish and humiliation than the memory of that dog's innocent face and frightened eyes. Still, I ask myself, "Who was that child? What was wrong with her? How do I learn to accept the memory of that young girl?"

A thousand rational explanations rarely atone for our feel-ings of grief, guilt, and remorse. Moving beyond these feelings is a journey of the heart, because that is where grief lives. I believe that one of the clearest paths to the spirit is through ritual. Thomas Moore writes: "Ritual is an action that speaks to the mind and heart but doesn't necessarily make sense in a lit-eral context. In church people do not eat bread in order to feed their bodies, but to nourish their souls." I believe rituals find a welcome seat in many people's lives. A regular visit to an animal companion's grave, lighting a candle in remembrance, creating a memory-album of photos and mementos—simple actions such as these can be a part of a wholesome ritual life. Whether we are grieving a loss for which we feel personally responsible or are simply navigating the dark waters of grief in general, rituals have much to offer. Rituals are conscious actions that encourage us to feel, to imagine, to dream, perhaps to settle into stillness and contemplation.

Wildlife rehabilitator Tina Hodge suggests that when an animal is crossing over to death, we ask it to take a message on our behalf. This message may give the animal purpose on its journey and can be as simple as "Please heal the animals" or "Help us to find peace." Many ancient peoples believed that a powerful energy was released at the moment of death. This power was thought to give great strength to the message carrier, enabling him or her to carry a message to the divine. This is one reason why many ancient cultures and religions sacrificed animals and humans in their rituals—to carry an urgent message.

After an animal dies, the task of tending to his or her body can be turned into a ritual. Perhaps brushing him or her one last time, decorating the body with flowers or a favorite blanket or collar, or simply sitting and speaking to this cherished friend can be part of the ritual. Selecting a burial spot, writing a poem or memorial service, making a grave marker, and placing the animal in the earth with your hands or scattering the animal's ashes in a special location are all powerful rituals that encourage us to absorb and digest the finality of death on a physical level.

Elisabeth Kübler-Ross, an expert on the process of death and dying, counsels families to participate as fully as possible in the hands-on care of their dead, especially if they have an urgent need to move through grief quickly and with a clear mind. Touching, bathing, and crying over our dead hurtles us headlong into the grief process and leads us to a healthy healing. We can participate in this intimate and nourishing ritual process with our animals. If we can actively and intimately care for the remains of a beloved animal, perhaps we may find the courage and creativity to do the same for our human loved ones.

Memorial services for departed animal companions can be filled with deep, personal meaning and provide another way for us to nurture ourselves during a painful time. One woman told me about such a ceremony for the death of her beloved dog:

> I wrapped her in her quilt and tucked inside a little wooden heart as a symbol of that part of me that went with her. She is buried near the spruce tree, where the robins come to drink and sing. My friend brought a miniature rosebush, winter hardy, and said it was a tiny plant for a tiny dog. And like Tinsel, it could endure the harshness of life. We planted it above her as we laid her in a grave lined with cedar chips.

One woman I know relies on a service dog to help her function with an emotional disability. The presence of an animal companion lessens her anxiety when she is away from her home. In the course of her life, she has loved and lost several of these dogs to old age and illness. An avid gardener and horticulturist, this woman has buried each of these departed guardians in her yard and has created unique and beautiful flower gardens over each one. "This is Jake's garden . . . This is Sasha's garden," she says. In creating and tending these beautiful gardens over the years, she stays connected to these important partnerships.

Another woman I met told me that on the day her dog died, she nuzzled his fur one last time. Later that day, she passed by a rose in her yard and stopped to smell it. "I thought, This rose smells as sweet as old Dan." Each year on the anniversary of Dan's death, she buys a single rose and reminisces beside his grave in the backyard. "I lost him twenty years ago, and I can still cry at his grave with a red rose in my hand, in honor of our last day together and his never-ending sweetness."

Our hands can pour out energy and grief. Clarissa Pinkola-Estés calls this process the "age-old craft of the hands." From the making of simple fetishes to the creation of elaborate sculptures, Pinkola-Estés states, "Art is important, for it commemorates the seasons of the soul, or a special or tragic event on the soul's journey." When my dog Keesha died, I spent a month gathering up every old photo I could find of her. As I assembled them, memories swallowed me up: Here she was the day I brought her home, a fat butterball of a puppy. Then on a camping trip in Wyoming, tail high and grinning ear to ear.

Now yawning as Old Faithful blasted off in the background behind her. I wept and laughed over all the memories. In the process, I pasted all the photographs into a big collage, which I then had matted and framed. I selected a poem to write across the top and had my best friend print it there. The collage has been hanging on my wall now for fifteen years, a source of healing and peace.

Writing tributes or poems to our animal companions can be incredibly cathartic. "When we lost our friend, Angel, I sat down and wrote a tribute, which turned out to be a form of therapy," wrote one reader. "What was more important was that I never felt I was writing it. It just flowed from my pen as I was embraced by feelings of grief and gratitude, back to back."

When people share with me their grief over the loss of an animal companion, I encourage them to consider creating an altar or shrine in the animal's memory. An altar serves as a focus for spirit and healing. I have crafted a permanent yet ever-changing altar in my writing office at home. It is a simple round table covered with treasured items: stones collected from a red rock canyon; branches of curly willow picked from my neighbor's yard in the spring; a twisted bundle of sage from my last trip to Wyoming; and of course, pictures and mementos of all of my animals. There is a small lacquered box containing a lock of hair from Keesha, Bear, Phaedra, and Arrow as a puppy. Small statues of wolves dot the table. The most treasured stuffed animals I collected in my youth circle the far edge of the table, their black eyes radiating back a lifetime of love poured into them. Before I begin writing each day, I look over at that table and ask for help in my work. Sometimes I light a candle on the table and read before it. The altar is a collection of images from my lifetime. I add to it, rearrange it, pack pieces of it away. It represents my heart and soul, and it brings me great peace and a deep sense of my center.

When my father died, I created a small altar for him on a bookshelf in our living room. On it stands a statue of a child with her father, a photo of my mom and dad when they were young clowning it up on a New York beach, and a pewter vessel containing a spoonful of my father's ashes. It was my animal altar that gave me the idea of a sacred spot for Dad, and both places are sources of joy and happy reflection.

There are countless ways to commemorate and honor the life and passing of our beloved animals, and equally countless ways to channel our pain, grief, and guilt into healing and healthy reflection. Rituals we create for ourselves have a special meaning. Take the time to sanctify and hallow the loss. Writing, speaking, dancing, chanting, wailing, painting, and singing our way through grief, we will meet our healing.

In my search for ways to move through and beyond losses that caused me intense guilt and shame, I stumbled upon *The Peacemaking Model* by Ron Claussen, codirector of the Center for Peacemaking and Conflict Studies at Fresno Pacific University. Although this model is used to help crime victims and their offenders come to peace with each other, I realized instantly that the three steps in Claussen's technique will help us come to peace with ourselves in situations where we have named ourselves the offender. The three steps of the peacemaking model are confession, atonement, and repentance, or as Claussen puts them: "recognizing an injustice," "restoring equity," and "clarifying future intentions." These steps can find their expression in rituals and processes that bring great healing.

In confession, we declare the details of our perceived misdeed or failing. My mailbox has convinced me that confession, or telling a story, is a crucial tool for self-forgiveness. In detailing the circumstances of an animal companion's death, those who write me frequently report feeling a special catharsis, a "kind of lightness." "For the first time since his death," one reader wrote, "I feel at peace having written this." In workshops, I encourage people to find a sympathetic, empathetic listener and share their most painful animal stories. However, it is essential to find the appropriate audience. Speaking about such pain and remorse to someone who doesn't love animals or who has a habit of being critical can derail the healing process of confession. Speaking these detailed memories out loud in a safe place with a supportive listener or pouring them into a poem, letter, or story are the first steps toward releasing the pain.

Several things come into play when we confess our story. First, the written and spoken word has power. Perhaps confession is a kind of circling of the events, a crystallization of the circumstances and emotions. Repeated experience has shown me that if I want to expand my understanding of something, writing or talking about it helps immensely. In addition, by telling your story, you begin healing others. Do not fool yourself into believing you are the only one in the world to hold such pain and grief. Those who hear your story have their own stories. Hearing another's guilt and pain reminds us that we are not alone. Finally, in confessing to your sympathetic friends, you may get some fresh perspective on your story. You may be reminded for the first time of all the good things you did for your animal companion; of the times you showed great care and love. Remembering this is the first step in balancing the shame against the whole of the story. And the whole story, which includes all of the joys, the frustrations, the love, and the regrets, is always far greater than the one fragment of tragic loss.

Atonement or restoring equity is the purpose of apologizing, of unmasking the aching heart and asking for forgiveness. If we cannot forgive ourselves, we should ask ourselves if our deceased animal partner would forgive us. In seeking atonement for myself, I have asked myself, "Would Bear forgive me? Lady? My chickens who ran free and wound up in the jaws of a coyote?" If the circumstances were reversed, would we forgive our animal partners? Frequently I have asked these questions at lectures, and people always answer, "He would forgive me. He knows I never intended for him to die."

Rituals for forgiveness include prayer and a conscious,

formalized request out loud or in writing. Whom do you ask for forgiveness? The universe, God, the Great Spirit, the Goddess, Mother Mary, your departed animal companion, the stars, the wind, your heart—whoever speaks to you. Trust your inner voice to guide you. Seeking atonement for his early days as an animal trapper, Roger Fuchs wrote this poem:

FORGIVE THE STEEL

O silenced ones long since unseen
Whose great and tiny bodies vanished are
Lurking in the earth somewhere
Elements again.
O silenced ones whose cries I never heard
Asleep in dreams
And cradled in a cozy bed
So safe and dry
While terror, pain, and agonizing death
Sprung out savagely in the night.
O silenced ones, forgive the steel!

O you who mourned in empty dens
Who lost your parents, siblings, mates
O young who died when care was lost
Forgive the steel!
Forgive the springs and jaws and chains
The death traps that I set for you
All for a moment's pocket change!

Forgive the steel of chamber, barrel, firing pin
Forgive the steel of knife and blade

Of plowshare, shovel, rebar, rail
Forgive the steel of screw and nail
Which take but do not give again!

Forgive me, long since silenced ones
Forgive me, and forgive the steel.

People write cards and letters to their departed animal companions. They compose songs, chant, drum, and burn candles
in their memory. Even as we move into the third step of the
peacemaking model, we will most likely return again and again
to the task of atonement. Asking for forgiveness is uniquely
human.

William Blake wrote, "Everything that lives, lives not alone
nor for itself." These wise words give sound direction for the
third step in grieving—repentance, or clarifying future intentions. These intentions will often be displayed in the form of a
give-away. In Native American tradition, a give-away is a ritual
of balance, of giving something back for what you have taken.
As a ritual for grieving, the give-away can become a special dec-
laration. What will you give back to the world to honor what
has been lost? The ritual of giving calls us out of our own clos-
eted, inner journey and demands that we return to the world
and to life. In Lady's name and as a way to atone for my childhood abuse of her, I have reached out to many animals in need
over the years. For the fear Lady endured at my young hands, I
have pledged as an adult to bring healing to animals in the best

way I can—through writing and speaking. When Bear died, I made a promise to his memory that we would always keep a place in our home for any stray cat that came to us in need. Since his death I have cared for and found homes for eight cats and kittens.

A woman wrote to me about her failure to notice advancing kidney failure in her cat. The illness came at a time when she was preoccupied with relatives visiting during the holidays. When her cat died, for which she felt at fault, she vowed to "make time, even if only a moment's time each day," to acknowledge all the relationships she treasured in her life. Another reader, after her beloved dog was struck by a car, wrote a poem that she shared with her church about the value of friendship. "I wanted to let people know, in Rowdy's name, how much friendship means, how easily it can be taken away if we aren't careful. I wanted everyone to know the importance of vigilance in friendship."

When an animal companion dies, our generous acts and gifts on behalf of other animals can serve as a memorial to the life of a beloved animal. Once when I tried to pay a friend back for an act of generosity, she said, "Pass the favor on to someone else." In this way we bring healing to ourselves and the world and honor to those who have been kind and generous with us. What better way to dignify the memory of our animal friends than to pass their kindness along through our efforts? You can of course give money or time to charities, but there are countless other things you can do. Put a birdbath in your backyard or fill a bird feeder; leave some nuts and bread for the park squirrels; rescue a lost or stray animal; walk the dog of a housebound friend; take dog biscuits to the animal shelter. Each and every small act of kindness moves us closer to healing our broken hearts. We can also resolve to be kinder in our human relationships in honor of having a healthy, loving relationship with our animal companion. As the song goes, "may the circle be unbroken": All acts of love and kindness come back to us. And so we give and receive in the same instant, all by extending our hands in love.

Bereavement is also an important time to nurture *ourselves*. Many animal shelters and veterinary clinics sponsor bereavement groups for those who are mourning the loss of an animal friend. Sharing the loss with a group of caring people who truly understand our pain is a gift of healing we can give ourselves.

NONE OF THE ACTIVITIES, reflections, and rituals I have proposed in this chapter are tools for avoiding or rushing past grief and guilt. They are offered as accompaniment for the journey *into* grief and guilt. As Sife eloquently reminds us, "It is often said that time heals all wounds.... A better statement would explain that what really heals is learning to live with the wounds. That requires time to achieve and complete." Only by our willingness to wade into the waters of loss and grief will we be cleansed. To achieve healing of so painful a loss is our task.

And this is not a task to be undertaken lightly or with the illusion that the passage will be swift and minimal.

If anyone ever again says to you in your grief something like "it was only a dog" or "it was only a cat," remember that each death is an education, an initiation into all of the other deaths and losses we will be asked to face in our lives. Each experience with death offers us sober and lasting preparation. Within the sphere of all living beings, *there are no small deaths.*

▼ ▼ ▼

Phaedra's Angel

It is impossible to tend as many animals as we do here at Brightstar Farm and not have death as a regular visitor. From the mice the cats bring in, to our involuntary donations of chicken to the raccoon and the local coyotes and foxes, we have more than our share of backyard burials. No loss in recent years was so great, however, as that of Phaedra, my precious llama.

As autumn settled in over the farm with its blanket of wet, fallen leaves and the east winds rippled through the back pastures, Phaedra seemed unable to get any better. She stopped gaining weight, remaining thinner than I would have liked. Her eyesight worsened, but she seemed unconcerned and managed to find her way around the farm with little effort. Sometimes I would find her out in the back pasture after dark, settled down comfortably chewing her cud. She had the good sense to stay put when night rendered her blind, and would wait for me to lead her inside her lighted stall and guide her to her food bucket. Always, Phaedra's calmness and innocence touched me. Her weak eyes would follow me wherever I went, and I felt blessed beneath their gentleness and warmth. In my mind's eye, she remained ever the shimmering, beautiful fairy, even though her looks brought giggles and caused visitors to raise eyebrows. Like most people, I could see that Phaedra's coat was tangled, that her legs were bent and misshapen. Because of her deformed hips, Phaedra walked like Marilyn Monroe in a tight skirt. Her face, with its once-broken jaw, was lopsided, and one eye sagged a bit when she was tired. Yet her generous spirit always transformed her in my eyes.

Twice that fall I had to lance open Phaedra's cheeks to drain abscesses that made her cheeks look like an inflated blowfish. Llama skin is tough as tree bark, and the only knife I owned that could pierce it was an enormous razor-sharp buck knife. The lancing process must have hurt terribly, yet Phaedra never once flinched as I slit open her infected cheeks and cleaned the mess away. I fretted about the coming winter, fearful that Phaedra would be entering a severe season with little reserve of muscle and fat. The winter would be hard, or so the donkeys' abnormally thick fall coats were telling me. As the weeks progressed, I did not see—because I did not want to see—that Phaedra was again losing weight, and that she was taking more and more time to finish off her twice-daily bucket of pellets.

When my first book began shipping to the bookstores in

December, my publisher scheduled my first extensive book tour to begin in January. I prepared for the trip by making sure all the animals would have enough food and supplies to last them while I was gone. The henhouse got cleaned. I filled the barn with fresh cedar shavings. The cats got baths; Arrow's long hair was trimmed from her feet and belly so that four tons of yard mud wouldn't wind up on our carpets.

No one could have predicted the floods coming. Soon after I left Brightstar, the rains came, and then the freezing cold and snow. Then an unexpected thaw melted a massive snowpack, pouring rivers of water and mud down off the mountains. When the rains and cold came again, they roared in on the back of an east wind that howled into the Columbia River Gorge with wind speeds of up to seventy-five miles an hour. Oregon rivers overflowed their banks and trees were pulled up out of the ground by the roots, smashing houses and cars and falling like monstrous toothpicks across the highways.

While Lee struggled to keep our home and our animals safe and secure, I drove from bookstore to bookstore, speaking about animals as teachers and healers. Privately, I berated myself because I was not at home taking care of my own. Meanwhile back at Brightstar Farm, a main water line ruptured at the Bull Run Watershed, and our community was suddenly without drinking water for several days.

Then the electricity went out. More freezing rain and ice storms turned lawns and streets into skating rinks, making travel impossible. Lee filled up the bathtubs before the water pipes broke and carried buckets of water to the donkeys, the chickens, and Phaedra. The yard was so icy that a crawl on hands and knees was sometimes the only way to get to the barn.

Each night after my book readings, I would call Lee and check in. "How are you? How are the animals?" I would ask. Always, he would tell me that everything was okay. "Is Phaedra all right? Is she eating?" Yes, he assured me. She was eating and drinking and not shivering despite the fact that the temperatures had been dangerously low. The winds had blown ceaselessly for a week and showed no sign of letting up. Lee had strung heat lamps in the barn and henhouse. Two years before, I had lost a fat, thick-pelted llama to weather less catastrophic than this. Each night of the tour, I prayed for Phaedra and all the other animals, and for my husband who struggled alone to keep Brightstar and our animal family intact.

The call came three days before I was to come home. It was close to midnight when Lee phoned. His voice was tired and strained. "Phaedra won't get up. She stopped eating yesterday morning. And she's shivering. I covered her with my down coat and two blankets, but the shivering won't stop." My heart cracked. We were losing her. I never dreamed when I left home that I would never see her again. Lee asked if there was anything else he could do. I swallowed a throatful of hot tears and told him I would call Mary, our veterinarian, who lives several houses down the road. I hoped that she could find a way to get out of her long, icy driveway and come euthanize Phaedra. I could not bear to think of my gentle, trusting llama suffering even one more moment in the freezing dark. My fingers shook as I dialed Mary's number. Thankfully, she was home. The roads had cleared up some and she said she would hurry to Brightstar and to Phaedra. I called Lee back and told him to wait for Mary in the barn, and to call me as soon as it was all over. Gently Lee asked if there was anything else he could possibly do to help. "Tell her I love her. Tell her she is beautiful. And just hold her tight for me."

I hung up, bent over, and began weeping. Phaedra had been losing ground and I had seen it and *not* seen it all at the same time. Our veterinarian warned me that Phaedra wouldn't be with us for long, but I believed that the strength of my love for her would somehow carry her through. Perhaps, I thought, I should have started tube-feeding her before I left to put weight on her. Maybe steady antibiotics would have kept the abscesses away. My weeping turned into a muffled wail: How could I not be there? Why didn't I cancel my tour and return home? If I had been home, I would have seen Phaedra slipping away before it was too late. I'd have started the blanketing sooner. With a turkey baster, I could have gotten some warm water down her throat. I thought of the shrieking wind and the black night and Phaedra under her blankets, chilled to the bone. Surely she was wondering where I was and when I would come to help her. I had always helped her. Now she would die without my help, without my hands to soothe her, my voice to guide her. In that moment, I hated myself. I recalled all that I hadn't done, hadn't been. The hypocrisy of it all: here I was, traveling from city to city pontificating about animals and love and healing while my beloved llama lay at home dying for lack of my care.

My mind slid back to Phaedra waiting in the barn. I realized that guilt would just have to wait. It was time for me to be with Phaedra in whatever way I could. And so while my body sat anxiously in California, I sent Phaedra my heart. My sobs faded and I willed my breathing to become steady and deep. Quietly, a misty vision filled my mind. I was home in the barn, listening to muffled voices all around me. I couldn't see well, but what hazy images I did see were cloaked in a golden light. Why were my eyes so clouded? I had sent her my heart, and she had opened to me and absorbed me. In the precious moments that followed, I was with her and we were one.

Breathing deeply, I smelled the sweet hay of the barn, heard the wind sweep across the tin roof while the shadowy figures surrounded by golden light moved around me. The voices seemed hushed and far away. I slowly realized the figures were Mary and Lee, and that they were whispering. Then arms surrounded me and the press of a warm body moved against my side. All was quiet, peaceful, and right.

The muffled sounds faded and stopped. Hot tears returned to my cheeks. I spoke heart-to-heart to Phaedra, telling her how beautiful she had always been in my eyes, emphasizing that she would be going to a place where she would be beautiful again, where she would live in joy.

In the next instant, my vision of hazy gold receded and was replaced by a wash of brilliant light that danced before my closed eyes like the fluttering of a thousand doves' wings. Into that swirling pool of light stepped Phaedra, delicate, sleek, and radiant. For the first and final time, I saw Phaedra as she truly was, as she had always been in my heart. Her eyes were luminous and shiny; her white coat floated down from her shoulders in a silver-spun cloud. She was radiant in health and spirit, intoxicatingly lovely. The hooves that carried her toward me were chips of the shiniest black stone. Around her nose rested a bright pink halter. Snapped onto the halter ring at her throat was a Peruvian-patterned lead of dazzling colors. Holding the lead and moving Phaedra gently forward into the light was an angel. I felt my heart fill with thanksgiving. In all her magnificence Phaedra waited before me, following my face with her eyes, tilting her small head, just as she had always done. For a timeless moment, I looked into the coffee-colored pools of Phaedra's kind eyes. Gently the angel indicated that it was time for me to release Phaedra to the care of her true home. She would be treasured and loved as vigorously as I had loved her in life. Then Phaedra and the angel turned away and the light dimmed, and I was once again in the bedroom in California with a phone in my lap.

In the minutes that followed, I prayed that what I had seen

had been real. When Lee didn't call, I began to fear that I was completely wrong in my imaginings. Perhaps Phaedra was still alive. Maybe Mary hadn't even arrived yet. A half-hour later the phone rang again. It was all over, and Lee was crying. Phaedra had died peacefully and quickly in his arms. "When?" I asked him, "When did she die? Was it only moments ago?" My heart sank.

"No," he replied, "I stayed in the barn for a while. Then I moved her heat lamp to the donkey stall. Phaedra died about forty minutes ago."

All the next day, I struggled with remorse and guilt for not being a better caregiver to Phaedra, for not being there at her death. I managed to torture myself thoroughly by that evening, in spite of my miraculous vision and the gift of Phaedra's angel. It seems I will go to any lengths, even deny miracles, to clobber myself. So I went to my final reading in California with a promise to atone for my imagined, inflated failings. Phaedra had been the sacrifice. My audience would hear my confession. Instead of doing a regular reading from my book, I read a piece that I had written about Phaedra many months before. It was a piece of writing that I felt truly honored her and captured her gracious essence. It was an agony to read out loud, but I have learned to trust the power of speaking that which is almost too painful to be told. When I finished reading, after the applause died down, I told the audience that Phaedra had died the night before. A wail arose from more than fifty mouths. "Oh, Phae-

dra! Oh, *no!*" Through my words, they had come to know Phaedra and her loving spirit. In speaking of her and in crying with
them all, I found the peace I was seeking.

When I remember Phaedra, it is as I saw her in my vision,
glorious beyond words, healthy beyond imagining. She is ca-
vorting in our pastures, her white head tossing from side to side.
She is wearing a pink halter and a lead rope of dazzling colors.
At the other end of that lead, holding that brilliant lifeline of
boundless joy, I dance beside her with wings of gold.

Saint Mac

by Jody Seay

It is time for me to get my own dog. For years I have only bor-
rowed them—from lovers, from friends, and occasionally from
the universe as a stray or two passed through my life on its way
to a permanent home. There is power in the love they bring
and there are miracles in the stuff that washes in on the wake of
that love. Not magic—magic is sometimes illusion. Miracles
are real.

McKenzie was one of my part-time dogs, a black Lab I
often babysat when her folks had to be away. She was not Lassie.
She did not save my life at any time, nor did she ever drag a baby
from a burning building, but she was braver than I would ever
be; we both knew it. McKenzie had the heart of a hero.

By the time we met she was already old, almost seventeen,

on her way to geezerhood and sainthood, I'm sure, for such was her spirit, as bright and pure and full of love as any bucket of sunshine that ever poured down on my life.

Cataracts clouded her eyes, but not so much that she couldn't see into my soul, comforting those worn and ragged places I kept hidden. Heck, McKenzie didn't need good eyeballs to see inside me. She was a dog—she used her heart instead.

Arthritis had locked her hip joints and slowed her down, but not so much that she couldn't take me for a walk or chase a slimy pink ball around the yard, rooting it out from the bushes with her nose, the only part that never faltered as she aged.

I loved the *feel* of her in the house and the sound produced when I patted her solid body. As I sipped my morning coffee, she would rest on the floor beside my own special corner of the couch, her sturdy head with its graying muzzle nudged right up against my foot—staying close, making sure I would not dash off without her. "Hello, big dog," I would say, and her tail would make one long *thrump* against the floor—just one—to let me know she was still here, still in the ballgame. "Don't you worry, Jody," that big, thrumping tail would tell me. "I'm still here guarding you and everything's okay. Don't you worry." I fed her and she guarded me; that was the deal we had.

When the medication for her jaw cancer finally weakened her heart and it was time to put her down, her folks called from Roseburg so we could say good-bye. I was blubbering so much into the phone I couldn't get out all the words I wanted to say to her—couldn't tell her how much I wanted once more to touch her hair, pat her on her ribs, or hear the sound of her tail making that big *thwhack!* on the floor beside my foot. "I love you, Miss Mac. You did a good job. I'll miss you." That's all I could say.

Miracles, however, often provide a second chance. Three days later, on my way out to gather the morning paper, I turned the collar of my robe up against the chilling drizzle of an Oregon November morning. It was still dark. Reaching into the paper slot, I looked to my right and saw, sitting perfectly still and spotlighted in the glow of the streetlight, a black Lab. Her gaze was fixed on me. The light reflecting off her coat looked like chrome. My breath caught in my throat and I stared back at her as the rain dripped off my hair and onto my nose, *The Oregonian* turning soggy in my hands.

I know better than to mess with miracles. If I had called her name or gone toward her, she would have disappeared into the mist, I'm sure, like some Scottish Highland dog right out of *Brigadoon*. I stared at her; she stared back, as if waiting for something. "Hello, big dog," I said, and smiled all the way down to the marrow of my bones when I saw that big tail thrump just once on the rainy street. I glanced toward the house and looked back to the street and she was gone, just like that. McKenzie, not still here, but not totally there yet either, had come around to be complete, to give me a chance to say good-bye the way we needed to.

Human beings are silly. We drop to our knees, praying for

signs and miracles, then try to talk ourselves out of believing what we saw, as if rationalizing it would make it any less true. I don't do that anymore. I can't. Signs pop up all the time like tulips in the spring. Miracles crash around me like thunderbolts. What I ask God for now is to help me pay attention so when signs and miracles show up, I do too.

Missing McKenzie is not enough, I've decided, even though I do, sometimes in an almost piercing way. Honoring her is better, which I do by telling her story, by recalling the look of her sweet face and how love oozed out of her whole being. She couldn't help it; love was her nature. She was a dog, but she was also a saint. That's how I think of her. Saint Mac, fresh from heaven, the dog who came back just one more time and fetched me a miracle.

CHAPTER SEVEN

Transforming the Relationship Between Humans and Animals

"The significant problems of the world cannot be solved at the same level of consciousness at which they were created."

—ALBERT EINSTEIN

"They're not my dogs! They are *God's* dogs!!" The young man's eyes looked crazed as he leaned across the counter toward me. Greasy hair and a straggly beard circled his angry face. Droplets of his spittle sprayed me as he shouted. It was a typical day at the humane society, where I had worked for four years. I was at the counter, receiving unwanted animals and relinquishing impounded dogs to their owners. This particular man's dogs had been confiscated many times, and always he would claim them, pay the increasing fines, and curse and holler at us. This time he had come to claim his Lab-mix puppy who had fallen into his empty swimming pool and broken her front legs. A neighbor heard the dog crying and brought her to the humane society.

On my side of the narrow counter, I stood with the vet bills in my hand. That's when the man leaned forward and started ranting in my face. He owned no dogs, he said. All dogs were "God's dogs." And he would pay no fees for "God's dogs." He began waving his arms in the air, then in a dramatic gesture dropped to the floor and pounded it with his fists. Leaping to his feet again, he leaned over the counter and started cursing me, clearly delighted at the crowd of onlookers he was attracting.

I said nothing, but felt the blood rush to my face. My mouth began to quiver. I pulled back my arm and in fear and rage flung out senselessly against him. My fist never connected, but my pencil flew out of my hand and struck him point-first in the cheek. He jerked back in surprise.

In the space it took for the pencil to leave my hand and hit his cheek, I had enacted in my mind every hideous deed I could imagine against him. For an instant, I think I even saw his head on a stick. He knew none of this, of course, just the sharp sting of graphite in his cheek. He flopped to the floor, writhing in mock agony. I, in turn, burst into tears, called my supervisor, and bolted from the room.

The young man could not possibly have known that in my

rage I never really *saw* him. What I saw across the counter was a walking, talking manifestation of animal abuse. Years before, I had lost the ability to see people as individuals where animals were concerned. People had become nothing more to me than caricatures. Those who cared for animals and fussed over them, I lumped into a general category of "good." Those who threw away their unwanted animals, let their animals stray, or refused to neuter their companion animals became faceless specters of evil.

By my mid-twenties, I had developed a black-and-white vision of the world, and my four-year tenure at the shelter merely solidified it. It was impossible for me to view wisely or with compassion the suffering I saw there each day. One day humane officers climbed the flagpole of a local high school to remove the body of a kitten who had been strung up by her tail and left to flail and die. Dogs and cats were deposited at the counter daily for being "too hairy ... too big ... too playful ... too shy ... the wrong color." I felt as if I were drowning in a bottomless pool of animal misery and human cruelty.

My moment behind the counter with "Mr. God's Dogs" remains painfully fresh. The memory humbles me every time I am inclined to say something trite and simplistic about what it takes to transform the relationship between people and animals. Because transforming anything is neither a small nor a simple task. Transforming the relationship between humans and animals has become the single most important vision in my life. The fact that we live in a human-centered world that treats other living beings with disdain, disinterest, and disrespect is no longer acceptable to me. It hurts too much. I want to see humans view animals with profound respect. I dream of a day when we will no longer use the word "resource" to define an animal.

Ultimately, my goal is less animal suffering. For innumerable reasons—too many of them based on economics or heartlessness—animals and the earth suffer at our hands. In focusing my attention on healing the relationship between people and animals, I heal myself as well. Furthermore, I am certain that the healing of the planet will follow suit: A fundamental shift in vision in any area of life ultimately effects a shift in many others.

Those of us who care about animals often carry painful mental images of suffering animals we have seen or even read about. I have often asked myself why I remain tortured by images of suffering I saw decades ago. What good does this pain do me? What good does it do the animals, who are long dead and gone? I believe I've found an answer that makes the pain of these mental images my honor rather than my burden. That honor is found in bearing witness. In holding the pain of another being's suffering, I honor that being's soul. And I carry within that painful memory, the most fertile seeds for healing that suffering. Witnessing the suffering of another is what drives us to seek transformation. These images of pain have the power to propel us into action and toward a more positive future for ourselves and for animals. A Minguass Indian saying goes, "The soul would have no rainbow if the eye had no tears." A woman told me of an experience that revealed how suddenly and unexpectedly we may be asked to bear witness:

> We were on our way to the cathedral when it happened. There he was, this blind man and his dog. And not just any dog, but a dog that looked like my own Misty reincarnated. Those haunting, heartbreaking eyes! The sadness in them was overwhelming, and I couldn't hold back my tears. Bless this man who had bundled up this old dog so that she could bear the cold weather. I gave him some money, but that didn't help the pain in my heart. What hurt so much was that people were rushing by him on both sides, oblivious to this man and his dog. I wanted to scream out "Stop, everyone! Look at you all rushing nowhere! Stop and look at this man and his dog. Are you afraid of catching this pain?" I will never forget this man and his beloved dog. Those eyes will haunt me forever.

Suffering becomes real to us through something that happens to us. Often it is an animal who gives us this harsh lesson. And often we are children when this lesson first comes. How these childhood lessons of hurt and sadness are handled within families and communities is of tremendous importance.

Because as children we look to our elders and peers for guidance: *What does my mother think of this injustice, this hurt? Do my friends laugh at this suffering? Does this suffering matter to anyone? Should it matter to me?*

One of the first animals who taught me about suffering was a coyote. When I was about eleven years old, a miserable, filthy, summer wildlife exhibit had been erected at a local park near my home. One of the luckless displays was a young coyote, his front leg mangled and still dangling in a steel-jaw trap. The coyote was crammed into a rusting wire cage with no food or water available. The enclosure was so small that the coyote couldn't even stand up, and he lay there day after day, covered in his own feces.

This exhibit was meant to "educate" us city children. Believe me, it did. I learned that many adults feel it is acceptable to enslave and abuse animals for curiosity and amusement. I relearn this painful lesson anew every time I go to a public zoo, circus, animal park, or aquarium.

Day after day, I pleaded with the park rangers in charge of the exhibit to care for the tortured coyote. They would not acknowledge my presence, nor answer any of my anguished questions. They treated me as though I were some annoying bug buzzing around their ears. I begged my parents to do something, but they were people paralyzed in the face of authority: If park rangers said the situation was okay, then their young daughter must be overreacting. I wrote to the local paper, called the town mayor and my veterinarian. No one would intervene. One day I called the mother of a friend of mine. Mrs. Roberts loved animals as much as I did. When I told her the plight of the coyote, she instantly mobilized into action. Within a week after she herself picketed the park for several days, the wildlife exhibit was shut down. The coyote made front-page news in our local paper, and soon after was released to the care of Mrs. Roberts. Her husband, a veterinarian, helped to care for the coyote in a pen she constructed in her backyard. Months later, Mrs. Roberts drove the coyote to the desert and released him back to the wild.

What this woman gave me is beyond words. Her courage empowered me as a child. She showed me that a woman's voice is a voice to be reckoned with. And she taught me that even though I was child, there was no end to what I could accomplish. She reminded me that although it was *she* who freed the coyote, it was *I* who had brought the coyote to her attention. At the age of eleven, I learned that one person can stand up against suffering and make a difference.

While I was writing this chapter, my editor, Maureen Michelson, returned from a long weekend on the Oregon coast with a story about her seven-year-old daughter, Alexa. It was a story about suffering, and about one family's courageous exploration of hurt:

Walking along on the seashore, Alexa crossed paths with a fisher tossing small silver perch into a bucket that had no water. When Alexa saw the fish flopping about in the bucket, their gills heaving, she was immediately disturbed. She walked over to where I sat on a blanket with her father, Gary, the two of us witnessing her discovery. I studied her face as she told me about the fish and their suffering. In that moment, I decided to let Alexa take the lead, let her feel her feelings and decide what she wanted to do. However, I must admit there was a part of me that wanted to rescue my tender-hearted seven-year-old daughter from her emotional pain.

So I acknowledged Alexa's concerns and asked her what she wanted to do. "I want to tell that fisher to give the fish some water," Alexa stated firmly. We supported her action and watched as she boldly approached the fisher, a tall, thick man in hip-high rubber boots, his jacket flapping in the wind. Alexa maybe reached his waist, but her courage made her tall. Breathing deeply, I told myself repeatedly, "It is the process, not the outcome. The process, the process...she will be safe."

The gray-haired fisher stood in the surf with his three buddies, their rough movements making the sea seem even angrier on that blustery day. Alexa stood toe to toe with the fisher and told him that the fish were suffering.

"Can you put some water in the bucket for the fish?" Alexa asked, fully expecting that this would not be a problem.

"No, it isn't good for the fish" was the fisher's gruff reply.

Alexa insisted: "But it *is* good for the fish." As she talked, her arms rose and fell and rose like waves filled with her emotions. The fisher refused to do anything and cast off again with his rig, ignoring her. Alexa stood aghast, in disbelief over a response that seemed nonsensical to her.

Head hanging, angry and hurt, Alexa returned to us, her touchstones. Alexa, a child, knew the truth, and the adult refused her truth. Alexa was angry, and I listened in awe as she so honestly and spontaneously spoke her true feelings. "Mom, I want to throw that fisher in the water. I want to cut off his head and see how *he* likes it."

A few minutes later Alexa decided to take things into her own hands—she would give the fish the water they needed to end their suffering. Secretly I cheered her on. With a determined look on her face, Alexa picked up her green sand bucket, filled it with water, and marched over to the bucket of fish, half of them now dead. She looked in, once again confronted with their suffering. But just before she poured the water in, she saw the stern fisher looking over his shoulder, staring at her, his glare as threatening as the Oregon

sea. She stopped short, his anger and size overwhelm-
ing her, and sat down by the bucket of fish and cried,
perhaps enough tears to fill the pail.

Her dad walked over to her and put his arms
around her. In that moment, I believe we all felt how
horrible it is to witness such obstinacy and unreason-
ableness in the face of suffering. The fisher walked
up, looked at the two of them, and continued to jab
more bait on his fishhook. Gary tried talking to him in
a friendly way. "Hi, are those perch? You know, my
dad and I used to fish and he always told me the fish
stay fresher if they're in water." The fisher grumbled,
and held his position: "No, that doesn't help." Then he
strode back to his buddies, holding his position as
rigidly as he held his fishing pole in a rough sea.

Alexa came back to the blanket and I held her for a
while as she cried. My heart ached.

When we went back to the beach house, we
watched out the window as the fishers packed up and
left. It was as if they waited for Alexa to leave first
before they would go home. I told Alexa that I believe
that the fisher had to think about what she said to
him. If nothing more, he must know she was courageous, and I believe he must admit to himself, if no one
else, that his day had been changed for knowing Alexa.

I wonder what impact this childhood experience will have
on Alexa. Will the memory of the fishes' suffering galvanize her
into action and activism? Will she hold on to that sense of

empowerment, standing up to the fisherman—the one in control—and speaking out about what she sees? Might she learn in time that the fisherman probably had issues of his own that day? In giving Alexa room to feel and to act and in validating her concern for the suffering fish, Alexa's parents gave her invaluable tools for reconciling suffering in her life.

Once a personal experience of animal suffering galvanizes us into action, what can we do to stimulate transformation in the world? I currently believe that there are two fundamental steps to this process. First, we must learn to make peace. By peace, I mean a deeply personal measure of harmony, serenity, and acceptance of the paradoxical nature of the world and our place in it. A colleague of mine received a letter from a woman who wanted to know how animals might be reconditioned in the wild not to eat each other. So strong was this woman's belief of death as black and life as white that she would rewrite the laws of life according to her ideals. No peace can be found in absolutes—that is, in black-and-white thinking. If we grasp at the dream of a world where no animal ever need suffer again, we will never find peace. Peace is found in shades of gray. In a culture that strives desperately—as I strove in my humane work—to label all things good or evil, seeking peace can be difficult. Peacemaking demands that we be willing to reexamine our perspective again and again. Peace asks us to have the courage to listen carefully to each other's stories, and especially to the stories of our enemies. Peace invites us to stand a moment in another's shoes and look out at the world through another's eyes.

Our second challenge is to become a visionary or vision-keeper. A visionary is one who sees possibilities rather than the status quo, one who can find new meaning in old stories, one who can help us imagine new stories. To master the ability to see beyond our current horizon is a lifetime challenge. Visionaries and their visions are often unpopular. For example, to save the dwindling salmon populations in Oregon, some people are promoting tearing down certain outdated dams. These dams cost more to maintain than they return in energy resources. Once removed, the streams and rivers these dams have blocked for decades could be reclaimed by the salmon. Yet the very notion of taking down something as symbolically substantial as a dam is beyond the ability of many people to comprehend.

Visionaries are often the first to suggest that we "take down" and begin again. Holding a vision is the very foundation of transformation and takes immense patience. However, in holding clear and positive visions, there is *much* we can do to stimulate the transformation of old paradigms. Saving endangered species began as someone's vision. Putting the wolves back in Yellowstone Park was a vision. The Endangered Species Act and the Wolf Recovery Program both support a similar vision: the sacred act of restoration, of apology.

To get a vision rolling, we must abandon the stale notion that one person is powerless to effect change. History and life teach us otherwise. Then we must concede that it is easier to teach an artichoke to sing than it is to create lasting change with physical or verbal attacks. True and lasting transformation never comes on the heels of threats or ultimatums, but in new ways of thinking about the world. Although I'm sure Mr. God's Dogs felt the pencil in his cheek, I know my angry attack did not transform his relationship with animals.

My personal exploration of peace—the first step in the transformation process—is constructed on some life-tested assumptions. First, I cannot work toward peace with another, human or animal, until I am at least *willing* to seek peace within myself. Second, I cannot work for peace abroad until I begin working for peace at home—that is, in *my* home, with my animal family, friends, and neighbors. Conversely, if I can achieve peace at home, I will have the tools to achieve peace anywhere. Making peace at home requires the same tools—in a more concentrated way—as effective international peacemaking. That is why home is such a perfect place to begin working for peace: It keeps us grounded, humble, and realistic in our larger peacemaking endeavors.

At home, I have looked for ways to make peace with the moles who dig up my yard and with the coyotes who steal our chickens. Often, I need to practice peacemaking with my donkeys when they feel abused after a series of vaccinations or a laborious hoof-trimming session. On a larger scale, I must practice a "good heart" with my neighbors, many of whom are happy to kill a mole on sight or aim a rifle at any coyote who passes by. Their views are at odds with mine, and it is easy for me to brand these neighbors as evil.

In seeking tools for peacemaking, I was dazed at the number and variety of techniques available. Many wise and spiritual people through the ages have addressed the need for peace. There are a multitude of definitions for peace and infinite ideas about how to practice peacemaking. In fact, some of these ideas are in direct opposition to one another. At first I found this confusing, but now I understand that there are simply many good roads to peace.

Because I am an incurably impatient and terminally busy woman, I lean toward prescriptions for peace that are concise, digestible, or action-oriented. "Little plums of peace," that's what I look for. Among the tender fruits of another's life-long inquiry, I have found a rich harvest. The Dalai Lama, Mother Teresa, Danaan Parry, the Peace Pilgrim, Rabbi Kushner, Elisabeth Kübler-Ross—all contribute delectable fruits to my peace cornucopia. These wise folk don't speak specifically to the human-animal relationship, but their wisdom can be thoughtfully applied to our relationships with all of creation.

His Holiness the Dalai Lama, exiled spiritual leader of Tibet, believes that compassion is our job and our mission, our path to peace. Many who follow his teachings believe that he is the living incarnation of the essence of pure compassion. This remarkable man was forced from his homeland and has witnessed the death of millions of his people at the hands of the Chinese, yet he has never uttered a word of condemnation against his persecutors. I have always been inspired by the clarity of his writings, but my delight in him increased when I read *Tying Rocks to Clouds*, a book of interviews with spiritual people by William Elliott. In this book, Elliott asks these masters to answer the most fundamental questions about life: *What is our purpose? What hinders or helps us? Why is there suffering in the world?* In his discussion with Elliott about the importance of developing a compassionate nature, the Dalai Lama includes animals and other living beings in his circle of compassion:

> When one sees that other sentient beings do not desire suffering and yet do indeed suffer, one feels very unhappy. All sentient beings—particularly humans but also all animals and insects—appreciate affection, compassion, and love. By identifying with others, one develops love and compassion. We can see the negativity in anger or ill feeling because it is harmful to others.... [It] creates a negative atmosphere in one's own house and destroys other people's mental peace and happiness—as well as that of one's dogs and cats. So you see, just one very short-tempered person within a family—someone who possesses ill feeling, for example—may destroy an otherwise calm and happy atmosphere for anyone who is in that family or comes into contact with that family.

A peace plum I embrace is: *Identify with others.* My own means for identifying with others is to search for some area of common ground between us. There is *always* common ground. Even if it is only a tiny patch of bare dirt the size of a fingernail, there will always be some common ground between us and "the enemy." Twenty years ago, if I had looked for some place of common understanding between me and Mr. God's Dogs—even if it was only that we were both human beings in a frustrating, painful situation—I think I could have left much of my anger at the counter and not swallowed it whole, choking on it for days. Maybe the man would have left the humane society with less hatred to carry home with him. A little bit of compassion might have brought us both some peace.

Sometimes in searching for a peaceful resolution to a personal catastrophe, it seems more noble to send compassion to others than to consider spending a little of that kindness on ourselves. I have always been my cruelest critic, my harshest judge. As I have practiced becoming more generous in spirit with myself, I find it easier to extend this compassion to others. Continually I remind myself, that I cannot find (or confer) peace abroad until I find it at home. Carol Mauriello, a former animal shelter worker, wrote me about a traumatic and heartbreaking event that happened to her years ago. When I read her story, I realized how healing it can be for anyone when we can summon up even a tiny shred of self-compassion in a bleak situation. Carol was only eighteen in the winter of 1978 when a fatal bout of parvovirus struck the puppies at the humane society where she worked:

> At first we didn't know what we were dealing with and felt powerless to protect the young lives in our charge. We cleaned and disinfected the walls, floors, pens, and dishes, all to no avail. By the time we learned the name of our enemy, parvo, most of the puppies had succumbed to its deadly embrace.
>
> How could this happen and why couldn't our best efforts make it go away? I was even more shocked when I learned that the community blamed *us* for the advent of this new disease! Did they think we had invited this monster in with open arms? Couldn't they see how hard we fought, how we suffered and grieved for every life lost?
>
> I didn't have a good answer to any of these questions. None of the old clichés about death being a necessary part of life eased my mind, nor was I able to take the fatalistic approach of "sometimes things just happen." My only solace was in my profound belief in the balance of life. Perhaps we need shadow to help define light. In those weeks, I learned a powerful lesson: Sometimes acts of courage and compassion can swing the balance back to a celebration of life. You don't have to be a superhero to make a difference. All you really need is a caring heart and a love of life. Even quiet tears of empathy for our animal companions' suffering can carry a weight that can tip the balance.

We made a decision to reach inside ourselves and channel our inner strength toward the bright and beautiful things in life. Even our simplest actions became expressions of supporting and sustaining life. Once we started to win our fight against the virus, the light of our smiles and joyful bouncing of the puppies guided our steps back to healthy recovery.

I asked Michael W. Fox, author and veterinarian who has worked with the Humane Society of the United States for almost twenty years, how he finds peace when facing all of the thousands of people he must meet with each year who do not believe animals are beings worthy of respect and humane treatment. He advised me to watch and learn from the "tea ceremonies" of animals: "Watch how they handle conflict. And see how they show kindness and compassion to one another."

Another treasure in my peace pocket is *observe*. When I observe the animals on our farm, I am humbled at how well they live together. They seem able to resolve disputes or set peaceful boundaries within their own family or species groups, and are adept at interspecies peacemaking as well. Pumpkin will share my lap with the cats, provided they keep a few inches' distance from her. If they move too close, she fluffs up her crest. Since the evening that Pumpkin bit Mirella's tail when the cat came too close, Flora and Mirella respect Pumpkin's space. Arrow defers to all the animals, down to the smallest chick, and she is one of the largest creatures in our animal family. She has shared her dinner with cats, chickens, and even donkeys.

Ozzie, our red cochin rooster died, leaving behind his partner, Harriet, a cochin hen. The morning after we buried Ozzie, I noticed that Harriet had taken up company with a black Polish crested hen and her rooster partner. They kept Harriet between them, and between them is where she was invited to roost that night and for many nights to come. Last spring, when a coyote carried away my favorite black silkie hen, her orphaned chick was adopted by a silkie rooster, who would even let the tiny chick crawl under him to roost. Consistently, I see that animals express honest emotions in each and every moment, and seem open to accepting new family members once they conquer their initial fear of the unknown.

Whereas animals seem to be able to resolve most differences in moments, I can take days. Watching my animal family is a humbling lesson in peacekeeping and compassion. Inspiring examples of harmony in the animal kingdom are acted out in yards and in the wild every day, if only we humans would slow down and observe. Ellen Bogner of Fort Atkinson, Wisconsin, shared her "tea ceremony" story with me:

> Our patio has become a feeding station for birds and other woodland creatures. Blessed with many pines and other trees, it also offers a haven of safety. In the evening, I put out bread and dry cat food to alleviate

wildlife raids on the neighborhood trash cans. In the evening, I take up residence in the recliner next to the window that overlooks the patio. A light illuminates the yard and I wait for each night's drama to unfold.

One night I was overwhelmed with what I saw. A stray cat ate the dry cat food while three raccoons sat eating stale bread a few feet away. As I watched, a skunk approached the group, and I figured that all the animals would scatter at the approach of this noxious critter. Instead, the most amazing thing happened. One of the raccoons moved to the side to allow the skunk a place to join in, and they all shared the bread. In a world that often sees these creatures as nothing more than road kill, I saw a glimpse of God's kingdom.

Lest this look too absolute, admittedly animals, like humans, are not flawless in their harmony. My three cats get along better with the chickens than they do with each other. Rather than compassion, the cats seem to depend upon space to create an uneasy peace in our household. We have had hopelessly disruptive animals in our home. Our rooster, Bogart, would exercise his spurs on every animal on the farm. When he began doing the same to the neighborhood children, we found another home for him. In his case, hormones spoke much louder than compassion. Ever Vigilant, the raccoon, keeps his delicate paws off of our chicken family because of the solid henhouse door between them, not because he is empathizing

with their fear of being eaten. In these situations, the tea ceremonies of animals are less than idyllic. They feel rather like an
impending barroom brawl. Even these examples of tension have
much to teach about peace: there is no such thing as perfect harmony, not for us or for animals.

A newsletter that explores the teachings from *A Course in
Miracles*, a Christian spiritual text, offered a useful technique for
finding peace in circumstances involving animal abuse. Asked
for a new perception, for another way of looking at abusers, the
newsletter suggested the following prayer or meditation:

> I bless you, I remember who you are.
> I remember the God within you.
> I remember *for* you. I see you in the light.

The wisdom I gained from this simple meditation is the gift
of *remembering for*—that is, remembering for people their true
and most sacred nature. In other words, I will hold the larger
vision for the abuser and for myself. Even if holding the highest
good does nothing to change the abuser's actions, I will have a
positive vision. This is far better than becoming emotionally
crippled, which is the guaranteed long-term result of sending
death wishes and resentment. Sending compassion, kindness,
and forgiveness at the very least heals the sender. This has been
an essential peace plum for me to cling to when I'm working up
a mouthful of venom to spit at someone. Years ago, an animal-
activist friend of mine went to meet her mother for lunch and

was aghast to see her mother walk into the restaurant wearing her new fox fur coat. My friend outlined for her mother all the horrors of fur trapping, and, after listening patiently, her mother replied, "Yes, I hear you, but to be honest, that's just not an issue I have my energy in. I'm sorry. I get upset about other things, but not that."

"You know," my friend said to me, "I have to accept that she has been a great mom, and that not everyone gets indignant or outraged at the same injustices. My mother volunteers at the veterans hospital and donates to child welfare causes. She is a good person. We all must pick our causes, and animals aren't hers." Her story reminded me of another of my friends: a pro-choice advocate in a family of pro-lifers. Even though this family disagrees at a deep level on this issue, they all remain close and loving. They recognize the highest good in each other, even if it is expressed in very different ideals.

A remarkable woman who preferred to be known only as Peace Pilgrim began an extraordinary pilgrimage in 1953 when she was forty-three years old. For the next twenty-eight years of her life, she walked more than 25,000 miles across the United States, spreading her message of peace. She carried only a toothbrush and notepad, vowing to eat only when offered food and to rest only when given shelter. This extraordinary woman touched thousands of lives during her walking pilgrimage. "My walking is first of all a prayer for peace," she said. "When you live your life as a prayer, you intensify the prayer beyond all measure." Through her example, I am reminded to live my life as a prayer for peace between all species to the greatest extent I can.

In 1997, the world lost a great peacemaker when Danaan Parry died. Parry and his organization, Earthstewards Network, launched numerous grassroots peace programs in many countries around the world. Parry's book *Warriors of the Heart* explores the processes involved in making peace. Parry's approach to peace has a down-to-earth simplicity to it. However, simple rarely means easy. One of Parry's most oft-cited observations is that you can't have conflict resolution without conflict. His writings encourage us to accept the discomfort, pain, and fright of conflict. It is only by walking the full length of a conflict that you can find a road to lasting peace. That doesn't mean that everyone will be holding hands and smiling benignly into everyone else's face when peace is achieved. Sometimes making peace means only that both sides will finally hear each other.

In *Warriors of the Heart*, Parry elaborates on a key to successful peacemaking. We must agree to *be there*. When animals' lives are at stake and the tension is high, few stick around. Some leave by foot. Some simply detach their minds and think of something else. Some turn to mindless, unimportant chatter to avoid the fear of facing the real issues. Some yell and threaten. (I've tried all these escape measures and more when conflicts arise in my life.) Parry recalled negotiating international conflicts that become intensely and dangerously heated. At those times he would stand up and say out loud in the midst of the negotiations, "I am *here.*" The words gave him the strength to stay, and gave the disputing parties the courage to stay there with him.

An event occurred at Brightstar Farm that showed me exactly what value there is in being willing to remain in the negotiations, to *be there* no matter how long it takes, and no matter how heartbreaking it may feel. This particular event involved chickens and dogs. The magnitude of this conflict was heightened because it involved my first book publisher, Maureen Michelson of NewSage Press, which originally published *Animals as Teachers and Healers.* She lived about three minutes' walking distance from Brightstar on the same country road.

Maureen had been my mentor and guide, and had become my good friend by the fall of 1995 as we were wrapping up the last drafts of the book and getting it ready for press. It was the first book I had ever written and the first book Maureen had ever undertaken with a close neighbor and neophyte author. For the book to succeed, we had to work as a smooth, well-oiled team—especially as the advance publicity began to kick in. Maureen and I, both strong-willed women, prided ourselves on our ability to work together efficiently and with goodwill.

The other critical parts in this drama were played by our chicken flock and by Maureen's two young and boisterous dogs, Thelma and Louise, who were just beginning to learn that the world didn't stop at their mailbox.

Maureen and I decided to share this story as honestly as we could to illustrate what can happen in any neighborhood, even to people with the best of intentions. We believe that conflicts that erupt between neighbors are no different from those that erupt between communities and between nations. When we talked about sharing this story, opening it up and looking at it in print, we were both apprehensive, afraid we would stir up old, unresolved feelings. In our discussions, we had to admit that we each remembered the event differently, and in fact there are points over which we still disagree.

I was in my house when it began: a tinkle of dog tags, a few surprised clucks, then a sudden and hideous screaming. I raced to the front window to see chickens flying every which way across the front lawn, feathers exploding into the air like fireworks as Thelma and Louise, free as the chickens themselves, grabbed mouthfuls of tail feathers, wing feathers, back flesh. By the time I corraled the dogs, with the help of a large stick to get Louise to relinquish one of the chickens, the front yard looked like a massacre had taken place. I recall that one chicken was dead and several were injured. To this day, Maureen remembers a great sense of relief that *no* chickens died, but one was seriously injured and died months later.

My hands shook as I phoned Maureen and explained briefly what had happened. Maureen told me much later that her stomach was churning at this turn of events and at the untimeliness of the conflict. She was suffering from a severe back problem due largely to work stress, and could barely walk. After offering me a sincere apology, Maureen told me that she and her husband, Gary, would fix the fence soon. Oblivious to the depths of my own feelings, I reassured Maureen that it was no big deal.

Four days later, I heard the clinking of dog tags once again and looked outside to find Thelma and Louise on my front porch. With them was Maybell, the yellow Lab who lived right next door to Thelma and Louise and strayed frequently. Now, it seemed, Maybell was enlisting Maureen's dogs in her escapades.

I panicked, then got angry and hauled the dogs home, thankful I'd been there when they arrived. Two more times in the next two weeks, I found one or more of the traveling dogs racing along my fence lines.

Our friendship was being tested. Although the entire scenario was about dogs and chickens, I felt as though my home and life were under siege. Looking back now, I understand the mentality that fuels wars and unleashes bombs.

Lee and I talked about taking the dogs to the pound if they showed up at the door again. I am ashamed to admit that in the heightened emotion of the conflict, it even crossed our minds to shoot the dogs. I decided to call Maureen and suggest a meeting with her and Maybell's people. Sensing that Maybell was leading the group, I believed that it would take all of the neighbors involved to find a way to keep the dogs at home.

Meanwhile, up at Maureen's house, Gary was spending

hours each day desperately trying to secure the fence around the pasture where Thelma and Louise stayed during the day. The dogs were becoming enthusiastic and creative escape artists. Maureen was nearly bedridden with back pain when I called. When I suggested a meeting so that the dogs would *never* get loose again, what Maureen heard wasn't an attempt at a solution, but a scolding. In a tense and frustrated voice, Maureen told me she could not possibly assure me that her dogs would "never, ever get loose again." There could be an earthquake, a tree could fall on the fence. Maureen felt that I was asking for assurances and absolutes beyond her control, yet another huge stress piled onto her already aching back.

For days, Maureen and I didn't speak. I feared Maureen had thrown my manuscript away. Maureen later admitted that she briefly considered canceling the book because she didn't want the hassle of the conflict. I couldn't imagine how we would ever reconcile.

But we were lucky. We had common ground—the book. Neither of us wanted to lose it. So we began to speak again— warily, grudgingly at first. For a time we spoke only of the book, what it needed, what remained to be done. The book became "safe space," the neutral soil. Somehow, Maureen found the courage to tell me of her intense hurt at being blamed, especially when she felt she was doing her best to solve the fence problem. I managed to tell Maureen about my disproportionate need for control in my life, assurance, and security.

Maureen and I listened to each other because we were afraid of what would happen if we didn't. Our commitment to the book and our strong desire to maintain peace as neighbors over-shadowed the intense discomfort, defensiveness, and anxiety the "chicken debacle" had brought down upon us.

Mysteriously, as we began to resolve our differences, the dogs stopped escaping the pasture. On the occasions when they did get out, they stayed away from my end of the block. The irony of this situation was almost laughable as we struggled to learn from our animals—all of this happening just as we were preparing to publish *Animals as Teachers and Healers*!

Thelma, Louise, and the chickens taught Maureen and me a lesson in peacemaking. We feel the foundation of our success was our willingness to be there—to remain in the discomfort zone for as long as it took. We also learned to value the process and to respect each other's boundaries and pain while we each struggled to cool down. And we came to understand that common ground is essential for finding a way to peace. Our common ground was the book and our larger vision of creating a world that is kinder and more appreciative of animals. Under clouds of conflict greater and lesser than ours, neighbors and nations descend into war. Because of our experience together, Maureen and I are both more empathetic and com-passionate toward anyone in conflict.

Another element of peace that I have learned from compas-sionate thinkers like Elisabeth Kübler-Ross, Rabbi Kushner, and Stephen Levine is that one need not be perfect to achieve some measure of peace. These modern-day sages reflect an acceptance of their own inner frustrations that inspires me to be a bit more accepting of my own. For example, Kübler-Ross, a tireless worker on behalf of the terminally ill and dying, feels helpless to stop her chain smoking habit. Rabbi Kushner admits to being angry and sad at the unfairness of life even though he has written a best-selling book about coming to peaceful terms with *Why Bad Things Happen to Good People.* Conversely, the Dalai Lama has achieved a sense of inner peace in the face of world suffering, but admits that he gets very upset and uses "harsh words" when staff members flub up on the job. Stephen Levine, who has been meditating for decades on loving-kindness, still gets angry and frustrated over the cruelty in the world. There are innumerable roads to peace, and we need not be flawless in our travel on any of them! Honest and vulnerable, these wise people show us that peace is a journey, a welcoming oasis, but rarely a permanent daily residence for most of us. Even in my barnyard, I am reminded that peace takes daily work. There's always the swift kick upsetting the harmony at the feed bin, the hard peck in a chicken squabble over a fat bug, a cat yowling to defend her rights to the bedroom.

PEACEMAKING IS THE STARTING PLACE. Peacemaking is the healing place. But then what? How do we achieve a transformation, a fundamental sea change in the way our culture currently envisions animals? In his visionary book *The Story of B*, Daniel Quinn says: "If the world is to be saved, it will be saved by people with changed minds, people with a new vision. It will not be saved by people with old minds and new programs."

Quinn uses the words *program* and *vision*. I have my own analogy of firefighters and rain dancers. When some metaphorical fire breaks out, most of us run for our hoses and blast away in a frenzy of exciting and ofttimes heroic activity. Firefighting is a program. This is all well and good and *necessary*, but it does nothing to alleviate the cause of the fires. It is the rain dancers—those with a sacred vision, those who see the blaze from a broader, more spiritual level—whose vision will ultimately extinguish not just one fire but all the fires. To put it simply, when minds and hearts are changed, people begin acting differently. Hopefully, they quit starting fires.

I remember a common bumper sticker from about ten years ago that read simply: "Think World Peace." It was a sentiment that sounded sweet and simplistic. That we could alter the world by our thoughts brought to mind another platitude: "Things that seem too good to be true are just that." But today I know that envisioning world peace is a worthy effort. I know that prayer works, and that thoughts have tremendous power. Scientists have conducted numerous controlled experiments that prove that the power of thought can affect a situation.

Rupert Sheldrake, former director of studies in biochemistry and cell biology at Cambridge University, has written a book that explores some of the extraordinary abilities of animals and humans. *Seven Experiments That Could Change the World* explores questions like: How do pets know when their owners are coming home? How do they find people who have moved and left them behind? Sheldrake has developed a fascinating theory called morphic resonance. He believes that the universe and the natural world do not run on changeless, eternal laws, but on memory and habit. A spider spins its delicate web, not on the power of some mystery called instinct, but on the strength of the collective memory of billions of spiders spinning billions of webs over billions of years. No doubt, the first web was a crude endeavor, but as more spiders took up weaving, it became easier for future spiders to build intricate webs. In Sheldrake's theory, it is the collective memory of spinning, which over time becomes habit, that supports the spinning. This memory or habit is what Sheldrake calls a morphic field. He likens these fields to the field put off by a magnet—invisible but incredibly powerful and incredibly reliable. Morphic resonance is the effect of these fields on people, places, and things: "The influence of like upon like through space and time.... Each kind of thing has a collective memory of previous things of that kind."

As far-fetched as this theory may sound, there is increasing evidence to support it. When a certain number of rats learn to run a new maze, all rats—even rats in other countries—have learned the route of this new maze much faster. In essence, the collective memory of the "first rats" guides them. Scientists have discovered that when a new type of chemical compound is made, it is often very hard to get the compound to crystallize. Yet the more often the new crystal is made, the easier this new compound will crystallize all around the world. Sheldrake believes that this is because a new "habit field," a new memory, is supporting the crystallization of these new compounds.

Sheldrake's work is inspiring and recharges my faith in the power of thought, both individual and collective. Suddenly "Think Kinship with All Life" becomes a credible plan. Perhaps when this thought becomes big enough or habitual enough, or when enough people hold this thought, the world will get on board.

I envision a world where animals and people can coexist in some form of sustainable harmony and mutual respect. Besides holding good thoughts, I ask myself, "What else can I be doing to help usher in such a world?" Perhaps when a critical number of people *live* the vision of a new way of life, it becomes easier for everyone to take part in this new life. As animals serve as inspiring examples to us with their "tea ceremonies" of how to live harmoniously and with compassion, so we can live as examples to others—examples of kinship with animals and with all of creation. Living our lives courageously can be our best opportunity to inspire others toward transformation. Mother Teresa lived what she believed, and by her example empowered others to do the same. Peace Pilgrim lived the vision of peace. And Mahatma Gandhi lived a life of peace through activism and nonviolent confrontation. We too can live a life that celebrates our personal vision of animals and humans in harmony.

Best Friends Animal Sanctuary in Utah is a good example of humans transforming their relationship with animals. Best Friends is the largest no-kill animal shelter in the United States, perhaps in the world. I used to believe that no shelter could possibly function without needing to euthanize some or even most of their animal charges. In my vision, a no-kill shelter would quickly become a warehouse for animals, where they would be crammed into too-tight quarters, maybe even stacked on top of one another. Imprisoned in such a place, these animals would live lonely, desperate lives, with no family ever to call their own. My vision of no-kill shelters included harried, exhausted workers, mountains of animal poop, and hopelessness at every turn.

Then I was asked to present the keynote address at the First Conference on Animals and Spirituality to be held at Best Friends Sanctuary. I arrived at the sanctuary with a sense of dread at the conditions I imagined I would find there. Four days later, I left exhilarated, my view of no-kill shelters completely transformed.

Somehow, against what I think are impossible odds, Best Friends works. It is a true sanctuary for animals, providing a vital, supportive community for its workers. It is a model of healing, joy, and positive action. And this sanctuary exists because a group of dedicated, committed people have held a vision for fifteen years that there *could* be, and *would* be, such a place.

Faith Maloney, the director and one of the original founders of Best Friends—and another fan of Rupert Sheldrake—explains why she believes the sanctuary succeeds:

> First, I honestly believe that the very ground here at the sanctuary supports us in this work. Best Friends is located in a beautiful red rock canyon, once home to the pre-Pueblo Indians. We know that they considered this sacred ground. There is an ancient tradition, an old memory of healing and of respect here. We also believe that the animals have a lot to do with our success. It is hard to describe, but we believe their loving energy supports this work.
>
> As a group of individuals, we founders started slowly with our own funds. No one person decided the direction for Best Friends. It developed organically. We are absolutely committed to the vision that loving and caring for homeless animals does not have to mean killing them for their own good. Our vision encompasses the importance of spaying and neutering animals, finding good homes for them, and caring for animals that "fall through the cracks"—the old, the handicapped, those who are sick or who have incorrigible behavior problems.

We have always been doers. We didn't wait for thousands of dollars to show up so we could start a new program. We started the program, and the dollars showed up. Of course it doesn't always happen this way. But it *can* happen.

The sanctuary is staffed with amazing people. We trust this place to select our staff for us. Those who join Best Friends and are not meant to be here simply move on. It's not a matter of having to fire anybody. They just leave because it doesn't feel right for them and they want to be somewhere else.

We have learned over the years that lecturing and arguing and demanding is useless. It changes nobody and upsets everybody. I believe we all go through that phase. But the only thing that actually works is living your vision, being a good example. At Best Friends, we work to be good examples of people who respect all life. Vision-keeping and hard work don't usually change the world instantly, but they certainly change those you touch over a period of time.

There was a prominent fellow in town who wanted to adopt one of our dogs several years ago, and we had to refuse him. It was embarrassing to all of us, because we ran into him in town all the time. A few weeks ago, he pulled me aside and said, "After watching you people for so long now, I understand why you felt I would not make a good adoptive home for one of your dogs. All of you have shown me how highly you value animals. And you have really made me think. I see animals differently now because of you folks and the work I've seen you do." That is the power of providing a good example.

Many humane shelters feel that keeping an open door policy is the only way to tackle the problem of unwanted animals. After many years of taking in all of the unwanted and abandoned animals in our area, we made a major decision to ask people to take more responsibility for the animals they were determined to unload on Best Friends. We did not do this lightly as the prevailing assumption is that if you make it uncomfortable in any way for people to bring animals to you, they will just dump those poor animals on the road and avoid the "bother." But we began asking callers if they had taken any measures to resolve whatever problem was steering them to Best Friends. Working with these people, we often found effective solutions that allowed the animal to remain in that home. People determined to give up an animal were encouraged to find the animal a new home with the help of our manual of guidelines for placing an animal.

Lo and behold, the animals dropped off anonymously at our door and around town *decreased!* We have learned that when you assume the best from people, they will try to give it. And in giving it, they will find pride in themselves. Our community has become much more "animal conscious" as a result of our living example of kindness to life and our focus on personal responsibility.

We believe that we have put something important into the universe with our intention and our efforts. No-kill sanctuaries are flowering all across the country, with each group adding memory to the "field" of this particular dream.

Best Friends doesn't espouse the "right" way toward a new relationship with animals and the world. Rather, it shows us *one* way. There are many ways. Best Friends demonstrates that there is hope for our dreams of transforming the world, because they are transforming a corner of theirs.

To transform corners of my own world, I work hard at peacemaking in my life, and I try to hold a compassionate vision of kinship with life. When the going gets personal, however, I can return to old bad habits *in an instant*. After the publication of *Animals as Teachers and Healers*, I got a letter from a reader who wrongfully accused me of letting people hunt on our farm. Stung by this attack, I threw my compassion in the backseat and—I'm not kidding—angrily wrote back that *she* should show more compassion. She wrote back and pointed out the irony of my response, and then reminded me:

It wasn't compassion that stopped the Nazis. Slavery was not eliminated without arguments and struggle—and death. People would still be working twelve- to sixteen-hour days, six and seven days a week, without argument, struggle, and death. The rights of women were not won without argument and struggle. What animals suffer at the hands of humans is a holocaust of unimaginable dimensions, a bondage and slaughter, rooted in profit and custom, that will be eradicated only with extreme difficulty.

As I observed earlier, although transformation can happen in an instant, it often follows a ponderously slow timetable. This is when fire hoses become necessary: programs, laws, bearing witness, holding accountable. Until our vision of reverence for life becomes reality, we are compelled to act in the face of animal suffering. Our dedicated action can take many forms. Environmental activism is when you picket against animal abuse, stuff anti-trapping flyers in the pockets of fur coats, or handcuff yourself to an old-growth tree to save it from a chain saw. Environmental terrorism, in my definition, means booby-trapping forests and blowing up animal laboratories and furrier shops. I am personally more suited to activism, but not because I am against blowing up fur shops and laboratories. On the contrary, it is because I am *too* drawn to these activities that I avoid them. Mr. God's Dogs still haunts me, and I know that I am still unable in many circumstances to keep from flinging that proverbial pencil. I'm afraid that I could easily go over the edge into violent confrontation on behalf of peace. I believe that the people who fight animal and environmental abuse in a confrontational or dangerous way act out for many of us—

certainly me—who would secretly like to rabble-rouse. They carry this energy for us, hold the memory of battle, and bear witness for those beings who have no voice and who cannot fight on their own behalf.

To be honest, how I feel about environmental terrorism and how I respond publicly are not always in synch. It is never easy to go up against the old paradigms. When lab buildings are broken into and the animals spirited away, I hear about the results on television and watch the newscasters put on solemn faces as they report how much monetary damage was done to the buildings. Frightening, dangerous, illegal, *expensive.* I know all that. And depending on the company I'm in, I may show less courage than I'd like and say nothing at all. But inside, I'm always shouting to myself, "Kudos! There's one for the chimps!"

While we work on our rain dances—our long-term vision—I understand that we must keep one hand on the fire hose for as long as necessary. The enormous challenge for me is holding on to my compassion while blasting away at the heat. I am far too tempted to hate the fire. Hating Hitlers, enslavers, and animal abusers will do nothing to transform the world. I believe strongly that this is in great part why we have made so little headway against abuse and suffering. You simply can't fight abuse and hatred with more abuse and hatred and expect to see positive transformation. Transformation never comes on the heels of verbal or physical violence. We can say no without hatred. Action can be—*must* be—guided with compassionate intent, or we will destroy our souls in the endeavor. Transformation through confrontation will be achieved only with compassion. Because I am not yet able to act consistently with compassion, I must choose my activism projects *very* carefully. Danaan Parry brings his considerable wisdom to this balancing act of action, compassion, and transformation:

> There is a secret that quantum physicists, Aikido masters and those who work with basic energy have known for a long time—change occurs when polarities are integrated.... For you to truly win in a lasting way, you must see to it that everyone feels, in some sense, like a winner....
>
> Our cause seems so obviously right, so immediate, that it is easy to judge others as "wrong" rather than to be of a different viewpoint. We are challenged to move beyond this win/lose attitude, to identify the foundation of common concern and agreement and to seek solutions that honor the opinions of others and fears of others and ourselves. Can you allow "them" to win, as long as you do too? Most people cannot....
>
> We must have the courage to say no when it needs to be said. But surely it is possible to see that "opposing oppression" is a win/lose position and can only, at best, lead to short-term solutions. If you doubt this, reflect on every war that was ever fought to secure peace and examine the long-term outcome for the

"winners" and "losers." Let there always be a yes to balance each no. Let there now be a passionate commitment to a positive future when our no's have had their effect. . . . We must accept responsibility for solutions that have no losers, even when our "adversaries" are unwilling to participate in this. We now have the choice. And I choose YES.

There *is* a time and a place to stand and fight against a world that denies animals a place at the table of life. As Parry said, we must sometimes say no before we can get to a mutual peace, a yes. Some of us fight the wrong people or fight before we've tried more peaceful options. Some of us never stand up at all. Sometimes compassion breaks down and all we are left with is a handful of animals saved or a tree spared, and raging anger and bitterness on all sides. And sometimes this is the most that can be achieved *at that time.*

The gift of a world kinder to animals comes in many wrappings, all of them complex, none of them completely tidy and unsoiled. On paper, it is easy to create absolutes, but I know better. Few circumstances in life are satisfyingly black and white. The following story is a good indication of how life, over the years, can go gray on you.

When I was eight, I won a humane society art contest. Part of the prize was a tour of the facilities. For some reason that defies logic, we young prizewinning children were escorted with our parents into the back rooms to see the animals who would *not* be put up for adoption. In this sad and silent collection, I spotted a nest of abandoned newborn kittens nestled in a shoebox. When I asked our tour guide what was to become of these kittens, I was told they would be put to death because they were far too young to live without their mother's care. Then and there, I began lobbying my mother for those kittens. "I can save them," I implored. All it would take was a bottle and some milk. Never mind that I had to go to school each day: I'd take them along. "Why should the kittens have to die? They've done no harm!" By the end of the tour, I was hysterical, sobbing. *Such innocent lives,* I thought. *I could save them all. I can do this! Just let me do this!* We went home without the kittens, and I was inconsolable for days. That those tiny, sweet animals were condemned to die for what seemed to be no good reason was beyond my understanding. The shelter people were clearly evil, I decided. So was my mother.

Thirty-six years later, I sit in my den, contemplating the concept of transforming the relationship between people and animals. The phone rings. It is my mother. She is calling to tell me about a litter of six newborn kittens she has found under a bush in her yard. My seventy-four-year-old mother cares for about eight feral cats in her yard, trapping those she can, getting them spayed and neutered, and releasing them back to her yard. It seems she is always one female behind, and then the kittens come. This litter has been abandoned by the mother. The kittens are weak and starved, and underdeveloped for their age. My mom asks me what can be done for them. Should she get some food? Bottle-feed them? "The poor things, so innocent, so helpless," she says with tears in her voice. I suspect that the mother cat sensed her kittens were not well. Hesitating only briefly, I tell Mom to call the humane society and have them euthanized. Over the years, I've learned what it takes to raise infant kittens, especially weak and sickly ones. Now I am afraid that my mother, in caring for them, will have a negative impact on her own health. Besides, Mom has exhausted her supply of potential kitten homes with the two previous feral litters she raised in her bathroom. So Mom does as I advise, and cries for the rest of the day.

After that phone call, I ask myself, "Who do I point to in my quest for easy answers, in my search for the the evil one? Does the finger point to me? Is there something more I can do?" In circumstances like these, a search for inner peace and personal balance becomes imperative, or else I judge myself too harshly. We cannot be all things to all beings at all times. In any given scenario of animal suffering, my ability to act will be tempered by other elements in my life: my energy level, my health, monetary circumstances, fears. We must continuously extend compassion to ourselves if we are to learn to live with doubt, confusion, and life in all its brilliance and brutality.

IN MY HASTE to "fix" life, small victories can easily go unseen and uncelebrated. For the past year, I have forgotten to congratulate myself for a hundred little "peaces" between my next-door neighbor and me: "peaces" that may reconcile a difficult situation. For example, this morning I heard the neighbor's dog, Tisha, barking in an unusual, ceaseless little yap. When I peered through our hedge, I saw that her cable was tangled around a tree and no one was home. Tisha has lived on that cable for a year. Her people have no fence, and she roams if left loose. I hear her cry sometimes, a sad, moaning wail floating up over the fence line when her people are away at work. It hurts me to see a dog cabled day after day. No, it kills me. When our neighbors first moved in and put Tisha on the cable line, I instantly hated them. *Evil people,* I thought. *Absolutely.*

I said nothing about the dog, but as I grew to know her people, John and Kathy, they told me how they had found Tisha in a sack by the side of the road, dumped out by a moving car and left for dead. Their kids love her, and so do John and Kathy. Tisha, they tell me in exasperation, can escape any fence ever constructed.

Over the summer months, John gave us vegetables from his garden, and we gave him fresh chicken eggs. He asks if his shop music is too loud, or if Tisha's barking bothers us. When our rooster crows regularly at four in the morning, John and Kathy turn a deaf ear. They welcome the visits of our free-roaming chickens, who can wreak havoc on young garden plants. "Good buggers!" they said. "They sure help keep the slugs down!" We have become good neighbors, sharing jokes and comments about the weather over our common fence line. They are not evil people.

However, I still fret daily over Tisha's plight. This morning when I heard her pitiful barking, I climbed the fence and untangled her. Then I played with her for a while and left her with a new rawhide bone to pass the lonely day. She seemed happy, and I felt momentarily relieved. "Soon, soon," I tell myself, "I will speak to John about Tisha." In the meantime, I will practice saying, "John, it just breaks my heart to see Tisha so confined. What can we do about it?" This is not something I could have said before now. A kind of peace exists now between John, Kathy, and me. We built a neighborliness, a relationship, slowly with eggs and vegetables passed over the fence. We have created common ground built on weekends of jokes about the wind and the summer dust, and a mutual need to be good neighbors. I hope it is a peace now sturdy enough to serve Tisha in some good way. Perhaps together we will build a miracle fence that will keep Tisha home. Maybe the kids will take her walking more. Or maybe John and Kathy will get angry with me and shut Tisha up in the garage or give her away. It would be cowardly of me to try to assure you that peace involves no risk. We know better. I don't have all the answers, but I do know that difficult situations can be ameliorated with loving compassion, common ground, and patience. These attributes give me hope for transforming the relationship between human- and animalkind, and, ultimately, between humankind and all of life.

If you haven't already begun, you can start transforming the world today by passing peace eggs and veggies over your fence lines. Strive to secure peace for the animals in your neighborhoods with gifts of listening sprinkled with a few good jokes about your own brand of local weather. In a world waiting to surprise us with riddles of duality and irony, and with confounding boulders blocking every turn in life's river, I pray that you will find your own precious ways to say yes.

> I say YES to my life
> I say YES to love
> I say YES to a one-world-family
> I say YES to all the children everywhere
> I say Yes to us
> I want my next act to increase the YES in the world.
> —DANAAN PARRY

▼ ▼ ▼

Raindrop

"If she lives, I want to call her Raindrop," Dawn said as she stood with me over the tiny, soaking wet calf that lay motionless on a burlap sack on her living room floor. My neighbor Dawn and her husband, Dan, had first noticed the tiny calf stretched out in the field across the street when they returned from church that afternoon. In the bitter cold pasture, they saw the calf's mother, hunched against a wild Oregon spring storm, bent down and licking her newborn, who offered no response. Dawn had no idea how long the calf had lain there, pelted by the sting of hail and freezing rain, whipped by forty-five-mile-an-hour winds that blew out of the Gorge with a ferocity that bent the huge hemlocks and snapped the necks off cedars. Dan put on his slicker and went out to retrieve the newest spring arrival on our block. Then they called me.

Atop the burlap sack, Raindrop lay unmoving, her limbs outstretched, her blue tongue protruding from ice-white lips. Her dark eyes were vacant and staring. I touched her muddy side and she felt like hard clay. When I bent to rub her with the burlap, I realized that she was frozen beyond the ability to even shiver. Her legs were rigid with cold, her ears like brittle icicles. "Oh, you poor, poor little one." I stroked her tiny face, no larger than the palm of my hand. Not only was she near death with cold, she was about the smallest calf I'd ever seen. I asked Dawn's daughter, Sara, to call my husband and tell him to bring over a nipple and bottle and a stack of old blankets. For all of us, huddled together under the halo of Raindrop's suffering, the next few hours would take on an almost magical, glowing warmth of community, purpose, and giddy exhilaration as we fought together to bring the small calf back from the edge of death.

Dawn ran to the bathroom and began filling the old white

porcelain tub with warm water. I carried Raindrop in and immersed her up to her neck in the healing warmth. The water turned brown as the mud spilled off her body. For the next hour, we women rubbed and sang life back into the calf. We celebrated when her white lips finally began to turn a soft pink, and thrilled when her stick-like legs began to bend and flex and push against the sides of the tub. Inserting my fingers into Raindrop's mouth, I let go a sigh of relief when her tongue began to feel less like a lump of ice and more like a dish of warm pudding.

Meanwhile, Dan and Lee searched the neighborhood for a source of calf colostrum. They called several dairies, toyed with the idea of milking out Raindrop's mother—a wild cow in a pasture of wild cows—and finally found a local farmer with a bucket of frozen colostrum, or first milk. The search took several hours. By this time, Raindrop was settled in Sara's lap while we all took turns with the blow dryer and fluffed the calf's now-gleaming coat to a glossy brown and white. Raindrop settled onto a thick, flannel-lined sleeping bag as we continued rubbing her, cooing to her, and encouraging her to stand. She struggled to her knees, but was too weak to stay up long, and slipped back to the customary posture of a newborn: head down and stretched out, legs tight beneath her narrow body.

We left extended messages on her owner's answering machine, telling him of our successful "rescue" and inviting him to come by and pick up his newest baby. Raindrop had drained several bottles of milk, and seemed to be enjoying the luxury of the heated bathroom. Dawn's friends and relatives began streaming by to take pictures of the calf. Satisfied, Lee and I returned home, exhausted by a job well done.

A few hours later, Dawn called. The rancher had come to claim his calf, and it seems he was not happy about us "interfering." The rancher explained to Dawn that he had seen the calf at six o'clock that morning, fighting to stand in the pelting rain, and had felt that the tiny calf wasn't strong or large enough to survive. He had gone out of town for the day and left the calf in the pasture, figuring that the weather and the coyotes would finish her off quickly.

My stomach clenched in a hard fist. Dawn and her husband had found Raindrop at one that afternoon. The calf had been struggling against the storm for seven brutal hours.

The rancher offered the calf to Dawn, who, other than the bathroom, had no place to keep her. In a tense moment, he stuffed Raindrop under his arm and left. Dawn and her family felt terrible. The whole, enchanted day deflated in an instant. I put down the phone, shell-shocked, and felt the anger rise up hot in my stomach. My mind was on Raindrop and her agonizing morning of cold. What kind of a person could leave a newborn anything in the sleet and wind and go off to a family feast? I began my mental assassination process.

Dawn had told me that she feared the rancher was taking Raindrop back to his barn to shoot her, because caring for her would be an effort. In the next twenty minutes, Dawn and I made dozens of calls to the neighbors and located a family that was eager to take on bottle-feeding the calf. We called the rancher's home and spoke to his wife. He had not returned from the barn, and his wife held little hope that Raindrop was still living. She said she would call us as soon as he came in.

We waited by our phones for the next hour, sick with worry and anger. Outside, the wind roared and the night skies turned black and lonely. When the rancher finally called Dawn back, it was to say that Raindrop and her mother had been successfully reunited and that, with minimal help, Raindrop was able to stand up and nurse at her mother's side! Both cow and calf were resting on straw in the barn and all was well. The next day, the rancher came visiting Dawn and her family with a big box of candy and an apology. Raindrop was doing just fine, he said. We had all done a good job.

It took me weeks to get over my outrage at the rancher. Spring was just beginning. There would be other calves like Raindrop. When I mentioned the incident to Mary, my vet, she offered me the view from the other end of the block. She reminded me that this man had been a rancher for many years. As he grew older, spring and birthing season became harder and harder for him. How many nights of sleep had he lost over the years to such fragile, hopeless calves? He was tired, and he saw his cattle as a business venture. The weak ones usually died very quickly. Not many years back, human babies were operated on without anesthesia because doctors believed their pain sensors weren't developed at birth. Why should this rancher think that a newborn calf had much feeling? He wasn't a "bad man." His dog slept on his bed. And he had helped Raindrop reunite with her mother.

Mary forced me, without knowing what she was doing, to find our common ground. There are times when I have been tired, and I have avoided many times going out in the storm. Years ago, my vet cut the tails off my Manx kittens using no anesthesia. I believed him when he said they felt no pain at that age, even though each kitten screamed and whimpered in his hands. After all, the doctor told me so.

If there comes another time when I find a calf abandoned in the rancher's pasture, I will try to find the courage and the compassion to call him and offer to take the calf off of his hands. I will remind myself he shares his bed with a dog he loves, and I will resist my temptation to make him one of the evil ones. But I will not allow the calf to lay there untended. Now I will practice saying, "Let me help. Let's work together on this as neighbors." And I will remind myself, as many times as I must to make it stick, that peace is an inside job.

Following the Deer Back into the Woods

by Shepherd Bliss

Driving down a dark country road about midnight, three of us peer into the unknown after a full evening together—Russell, his eight-year-old son Owen, and me. On the year's longest night, as well as one of its coldest, we are returning from a winter-solstice gathering high on a hill overlooking the Pacific Ocean in semi-rural Sonoma County in Northern California. We are heading back to the small town of Sebastopol after experiencing the mysteries of darkness, water, redwood trees, fire, and moonlight. We each gave up something from the declining year and expressed a desire for the emerging year. Having been outside together in the cold December air for hours with dozens of friends has invigorated us and our souls. Content, alert, and aware, we look forward to a good night's sleep.

Suddenly our car lights capture a fallen figure in the road. The first thing I notice is his magnificent spread of antlers. Immobilized, the mature buck appears dead. His rack points toward the woods and his hooves reach into the other lane. An awful feeling sinks in my stomach in this presence of death. We decide to inspect the deer, partly to show young Owen. We move slowly toward the wild brown animal. A shiver runs through his body and spasms shake his neck. I remember watching chickens on the farm during my childhood; they would continue shaking long after they were dead.

"He's still breathing!" the boy exclaims. One eye opens partway. "He's in shock," I observe. The deer's eye closes. Rather than being a dead deer, he is a dying deer. The awful feeling in my stomach deepens. A machine has struck down this innocent animal as he walked through the dark woods and wandered onto the road. "How long ago did this happen?" I wonder out loud. "Have others passed by, leaving him for dead?"

He is motionless, and we stand by helplessly. A great majesty has fallen to the asphalt. The once-high crown now lies scattered on an artificial cover—nature having collided with culture. Suddenly the eye we can see opens again, more completely this time. His tongue moves about uncomfortably. My eyes meet his eye. He tries to lift his head; it falls back to the asphalt with a thud. We witness his futile, painful attempts to regain his senses and stand up. I recollect the times in my life that I have fallen.

"Let's pull him off the road," Russell suggests. We move toward Buck. His thrusting, pointed antlers threaten us; we leap back. Stunned and down, he is not out yet. A single blow struck him down, but from his fallen place a wildness rushes in to intimidate us and to protect him. He bangs his antlers on the hard pavement. "Leave me alone," Buck seems to say. "Haven't your people already done enough?" I think of the earth and the damage we have done to animals, plants, the air, the water, and so much of the life that was freely given, which sustains us, and without which we will perish.

I am drawn to this brother. I want to make contact, many feelings rush in: guilt, fear, doubt. I do not want to hurt him further. Our intention is to honor the deer, dead or alive. We want to help, but he does not trust us. I remember that you are not supposed to move people after a car accident because you may break the spinal cord inadvertently. But what to do with a wild animal? I know so little about the care of wild animals. Our ancestors knew how to care for such fallen dignity. If he is not dead yet, perhaps we will have to kill him to end his misery. But how? Then we would need to bury him. What would a proper burial for such a king entail?

The boy, his father, and this midlife man circle the fallen deer, trying to figure out what to do. After what seems like a long time, perhaps ten minutes, a car approaches in the other direction, slows down, passes us, stops. The driver emerges from the darkness; a slight figure moves toward us. After checking us out, a teenager, under driving age, walks deliberately toward us. "I hit the deer," he confesses. Compassion, rather than anger, rises in me. This teenager is not much bigger than Owen. I see agony in his eyes and face. He too is in a state of shock. He is no more responsible for this collision than we are. We have built this civilization together, and all bear some responsibility.

I remember times I did not return to scenes of trauma, walking away, leaving it to someone else to clean up. Returning to finish something is important. Now we are four males in a council, trying to decide what to do. We stand in silence. Buck tries to rise again. We surround the wounded male—not us, yet one of us, a fallen brother. "Let's turn off the headlights!" I suggest, remembering that they daze deer. I feel powerless and inept. Witnessing the death of animals and humans used to be more common. Now it is unusual to see people die; we hide the dying in hospitals and "rest homes."

"His back appears broken," Russell comments. "What happens when your back is broken?" Owen innocently asks. "You die." Constructing a life takes years; dying can take less than a second. Dying is more than a solitary act; it is usually a social act influencing others. Who is Buck leaving behind? Who might notice my leaving? I wonder. What do animals have to teach humans about life and death? They do not seem to agonize over it the way we do.

We surround Buck. My feelings immobilize me. He seems bewildered. But with the car headlights off, the darkness increases and Buck's power grows.

We are in his world now. Russell suddenly crouches down, boldly grabs the antlers and pulls with all his biker's might. Buck flies off the road and onto the Earth. His body slides to the dirt and rolls over. The minute he hits the ground, he seems to wake from his slumber and struggles to his feet! Without even looking at us, he stumbles off down the road. He shakes his antlered head, as if awakening from a drunk or bad dream. His fallen figure is erect again, his shape having been shifted by Russell's forceful pull.

Now it is we who are stunned. Dying has been transformed into resurrection. Two men and two boys look at each other, eyes wide open. A silent joy replaces the sinking feeling in my stomach. We have witnessed a miracle. Life has returned into a dying body. Our slowing down, stopping, and intervening has stabilized a fallen brother. Images of other fallen males who never rose pass through my mind.

"We're glad you came back," I say to the teenager. He smiles and walks back through the darkness to his deadly car. He does not yet have all these dead and dying people inside him, who rise when I am in the presence of death. I linger in their memories, honoring them and our connections. The teenager now has this deer and his return to life inside him.

We walk to our car and follow Buck down the road. He is still in danger, as three cars pass quickly by. Another car comes, slows down, and stops. "Get off the road, Buck, off the road!" I yell to Buck. And to myself. Life can become death so quickly, whereas it takes more time to bring the dying back to life. Buck finally enters the woods. I release a great sigh of relief and feel the mystery. He's back home and may receive the healing he needs. Or he may die soon. Better to die at home than on the road. At least he will be beyond the gaze of the killer cars and humans. The giant redwood trees beckon me to follow him and join them. We stop by the roadside, watching the trees that receive him so openly. We linger, still stunned. Our eyes peer into the unknown woods that have welcomed back our brother. I wonder how well they might receive me.

We drive home in silence, moving more slowly and deliberately. I wake up early the next morning and lie in bed, immobile, for a long time—Buck still on my mind. I see his prone brown body and glazed eye, weak but glaring at me with a message. Men today have lost so much—being more connected to machines than to animals. Most contemporary men have lost the gaze of wild animals. Buck lives a basic, simple truth. Even while fallen, he retained his dignity and majesty, never becoming a victim. Buck remained strong, even in what appeared to be death. Deer wisdom is unique. Each creature has its own intelligence and helps form the whole. When humans lose contact with deer, other animals, and the natural world itself, we lose parts of our souls. Men's loss of animals and the woods separates us from our ancestors.

Masculinity in America has been stunned, shocked. By cars and machines. By industrialism. We men used to work mainly with our hands, connecting us to wood, soil, and friends. We need to follow the deer back into the trees. We need to return home. We are dying and need to reverse the process. We need to return to the woods for our healing, our medicine, our wildness.

A couple of days later Russell and his boy come over to play. Owen has been telling the deer story to everyone. I ask him what he felt as it was happening. "Half sad and half afraid," he responds. "I felt a pain in my chest, next to my heart." So Owen has a body memory of the deer. An archetypal boy-animal night has occurred for Owen. Now we all carry it in our collective memory.

Russell's fiancée Leslie adds another dimension to our still-unfolding story. "When the masculine has been wounded, it is dangerous to approach it. One can be hurt." So some people do not deal with it. Or they try gentle nurturing, which would not have gotten Buck on his feet. "It required a male approach," according to Leslie. "The bull needed to be taken by the horns." Sometimes one does the right thing, as Russell did with the deer, and a situation is transformed. Other times we are passive in the face of crisis. Contemporary masculinity has been so stunned by industrialism and other forces that men too often fail to take appropriate initiative.

The teenager's slight frame rises in my mind. Does he have good male mentoring? Or is his father absent, like mine, and like most men's fathers since industrialism? We have lost our animal teachers, like those who taught the boy Arthur, enabling him to grow into King Arthur. I am glad we did not accuse the teenage boy, blame or shame him, thus adding to his agony. He returned to see the deer rise again.

That which fell down rose up again! A good image for my

next fall. To live is to fall and then figure out how to roll, or how to get the necessary help to roll. The deer incident has changed me, more internally than externally, in ways that are not yet clear to me. I drive slower on country roads. I am more aware of the woods at the side and what they may contain. Some new consciousness has awakened in me. I have much to learn from animals and boys.

The Spirit of Brightstar

Early in September 1997, on a glorious late summer afternoon when the skies were blue and the fields yellow as egg yolks, I assembled an altar at the east end of our pasture burn pile. A sawed-off and rusty fifty-gallon drum served as a base. Upon it, I put a blue ribbon from the first donkey show we ever won with our "girls." Next to the ribbon, I placed stems and short branches from our most beloved trees: the hemlock out front, the maple on the back lawn, the cluster of mountain ash in the driveway. A robin's nest was added to the assembly. And a few tiny apples from the gnarled apple tree in the back pasture. From each animal on the farm, I collected a snip of fur or a piece of feather. This soft bundle I placed beside the other items on the altar. To the collection of fur, I added a few treasured hairs from Keesha, from Bear, from Phaedra. Finally I set beneath the altar a skinny red plastic binder that had been left behind by our farm's original owners. In it were pages of information about the house and yard: where the water lines were buried, the location of the fuse box, the size of the septic tank.

With masses of curly willow and dried deadfall from the last winter's storms, I erected the makings for a small bonfire. It would burn later that evening. As the shadows lengthened and disappeared into twilight and the chickens made their way to the henhouse, I touched each item on the altar, remembering, dreaming, grieving, and waiting.

It was close to ten when our friends arrived—two couples with drums, smudge sticks, wine, and matches. We walked through the dark barnyard to the burn pile. We smudged ourselves with the cleansing smoke of Oregon cedar and put a match to the fire. For the next hour, drumming, laughing, and crying, we shared memories of each other and of the farm. To the fire, I ceremoniously dedicated all the treasured items on my altar, speaking tearfully over each. Then, to our newest friends, a couple whom we had known only for several weeks, I gave the plastic binder and the house keys to our beloved farm. Brightstar had been sold. Her new stewards would take possession in less than a week.

The new owners asked that night if it would be possible for them to keep the name Brightstar, as they loved the name for their new home as much as we had. I said yes. Yes, because Brightstar is not so much a place as a vision. In the five years we lived there, Brightstar taught us unforgettable lessons of harmony, peace, joy, and childlike wonderment, and expanded our horizons to new worlds of thought and feeling. And so the name, and the vision, would go with us, as well. Brightstar Farm will continue to blossom in the Oregon hills, and would bury its seeds in our new home a thousand miles away. There is room for two Brightstars. Maybe, someday in spirit, there will be hundreds, thousands of Brightstars.

The decision to sell our farm had been agonizing. We were leaving only because of a dream that pulled me even more strongly than my love for my Oregon farm. In ten thousand memories, and in boxes and drawers and wheelbarrows, we packed away the vision and the spirit of our precious home. Those last days were a concert of tears and frenzied activity. When I wasn't packing, I was crying. "I must be crazy to leave this place," I said to myself countless times each day. Still, my dream propelled me forward. It was an old dream, granted, but unlike so many old dreams, this one had never died.

In the craziness of moving, we somehow made space for a

new canine friend for Arrow—a snow-white pup with feet the size of softballs whom we christened Strongheart. When we pulled out of the driveway for the final time, our car and travel-truck were filled with animals. Three states to the east our new home, a log cabin and three acres of sagebrush and wildflowers, sat empty and waiting. *You will have many homes.* The vision of my afternoon in Teton Canyon with Arrow was carrying me forward.

A few hundred yards from the house, Lee stopped to adjust something on the truck. One last time I raced back up the hill to the house and to the massive guardian hemlock on the lawn. Wrapping my arms around its rough comforting trunk in a last loving embrace, I choked out through my tears, "Please remember me." Then I hurried back to the car, pulled in behind the overstuffed truck, and headed down the hill toward Jackson Hole, Wyoming.

Books

Andrews, Ted. *Animalspeak.* Great guidebook into the realm of totem animals.

Caras, Roger. *A Perfect Harmony.* A journey into the domestication of animals. What it meant for humans and what is has meant for the animal kingdom.

Dalai Lama. *The Power of Compassion.* Wonderful little guide to compassionate living.

Earle, Sylvia. *Sea Change: A Message of the Oceans.* To quote from the cover: "What Rachel Carson was to insecticides, birds, and our planet in 1962, Sylvia Earle ... is now to the oceans."

Elliott, William. *Tying Rocks to Clouds.* Enlightening, inspirational interviews with many of the most recognized spiritual leaders of our time. The honesty and humor these sages share with Elliott is refreshing and courageous. A real upper!

Fox, Matthew, and Rupert Sheldrake. *Natural Grace.* Stimulating dialogue between a maverick priest and a maverick scientist. A fascinating blending of both views.

Fox, Michael. *Eating with Conscience: The Bioethics of Food.* Must reading for everyone who eats! This book tackles a complex subject with compassion, good science, and a blessed lack of gore.

Grandin, Temple. *Thinking in Pictures and Other Reports from My Life with Autism.* International speaker and creator of humane livestock-handling equipment, Grandin—autistic since birth—speaks of her unique vision of the world. Grandin speculates that perhaps she sees the world much as cattle might: in mental pictures.

Hiby, Lydia, and Bonnie S. Weintraub. *Conversations with Animals:*

Cherished Messages and Memories as Told by an Animal Communicator. A wonderful, enlightening book by a remarkable animal communicator.

Hillman, James. *The Soul's Code.* An excellent exploration of how we are "called" by our souls to passions in our lives.

Hogan, Linda, Deena Metzger, and Brenda Peterson, eds. *Intimate Nature: The Bond Between Women and Animals.* An intimate look at the special relationship women have formed with animals.

Linn, Denise. *The Secret Language of Signs.* Wonderful exploration into the meaning of events, and how the hands of the gods touch us through signs and omens.

Martin, Ann. *Food Pets Die For: Shocking Facts About Pet Food.* Brilliantly researched exploration of what goes into pet food. Readable, alarming, urgent. Includes wonderful recipes for homemade pet food.

Masson, Jeffrey Moussaieff. *When Elephants Weep* and *Dogs Never Lie About Love.* Masson speaks directly, fearlessly, and compassionately about the emotional lives of animals.

Moore, Thomas. *The Re-Enchantment of Everyday Life.* An inspirational exploration into enchantment: what it is, how it touches us, and how to bring more of it into our everyday lives.

Parry, Danaan. *Warriors of the Heart.* A peacemaking bible by the late, great international peacemaker. Filled with practical suggestions for conflict resolution on a personal as well as a planetary level.

Quinn, Daniel. *Ishmael; Providence; The Story of B; My Ishmael.* Words cannot express what these books have meant to me. Quinn's works showed me a vision of human history that completely transformed my view of life, and what it means to be human. Please read these.

Remen, Rachel Naomi. *Kitchen Table Wisdom.* This is a book of healing stories told by one of the most gifted healers it has ever been my privilege to know.

Roads, Michael. *Talking with Nature; Journey into Nature; Journey into Oneness.* Roads's relationship with nature is a deeply personal and intensely spiritual one. These books delve into the concept of nature as teacher and healer.

Sams, Jamie, and David Carson. *Medicine Cards.* Available at many bookstores. Comes with a set of animal cards and a beautiful animal totem guidebook.

Siegel, Bernie. *Love, Medicine and Miracles.* More than any other writer on the subject of cancer and healing, Siegel gave me great hope and courage.

Traisman, Enid. *My Personal Pet Remembrance Journal.* A healing workbook that guides one gently through the loss of a beloved animal companion. An excellent gift for a grieving friend or for yourself.

Other Resources

ANAFLORA
Sharon Callahan is an animal communicator and healer who has developed a unique line of flower essence therapy for animals. She also works with those grieving the loss of an animal companion. Her work is gentle, intuitive, and highly effective. Write: POB 1056, Mount Shasta, CA 96067, or call: 530-926-6424. Website: www.anaflora.com.

BEST FRIENDS ANIMAL SANCTUARY
The largest no-kill animal sanctuary in the United States, Best Friends is filled with hope, joy, and spirit. They care for 1,500 homeless animals daily, produce a marvelous and upbeat magazine, and offer many outreach education and training services. Write: Best Friends Sanctuary, Kanab, Utah 84741-5001, or call: 801-644-2001. Website: www.Bestfriends.org.

COUNCIL OF ALL BEINGS
This empowering and transformational workshop is conducted all over the world by trained facilitators. To find one in your area, contact: John Seed, Rainforest Information Centre, POB 368, Lismore, NSW 2480, Australia. Or e-mail John Seed at: jseed@peg.apc.org.

DELTA SOCIETY
The best source for information about pet-assisted therapy and service animals. Also, they publish a wonderful magazine, *Interactions,*

that explores the human-animal bond. For information, write: 289 Perimeter Road East, Renton, WA 98055, or call: 425-226-7357. Website: www.Deltasociety.org.

THE ELEPHANT SANCTUARY AT HOHENWALD
Zoos and circuses are required, under international regulations for endangered and exotic species, to provide for such animals until their death. Because elephants may live to the age of seventy, careful provision must be made for their long-term care. As an endangered species, Asian elephants are entitled to protection. As highly intelligent animals who have spent their lives serving and entertaining mankind, they are especially deserving of our compassion and respect. For more information, contact: Carol Buckley, POB 393, Hohenwald, Tennessee 38462. Or call: 615-796-6500.

YES! A JOURNAL OF POSITIVE FUTURES
This is a vision keeper's dream come true—founded on the work of the late Danaan Parry. For information, write: POB 10818, Bainbridge Island, WA 98110-0818. Website: www.futurenet.org.

A former technical writer and editor, SUSAN CHERNAK McELROY has enjoyed a lifelong love affair with animals. Her writing is featured in several anthologies, including *Intimate Nature: The Bond Between Women and Animals*, coedited by Brenda Peterson, Linda Hogan, and Deena Metzger; *Kinship with the Animals*, by Michael Tobias and Kate Solisti Mattelson; *Wounded Healers*, by Rachel Naomi Remen, and *Chicken Soup for Soul Survivors*, by Jack Canfield and Mark Hansen. She lives with her husband and animal family on a small farm in Jackson Hole, Wyoming, named Brightstar.

McElroy offers lectures, audiotapes, and workshops on the human-animal relationship. You may reach her at her website: www.brightstar-farm.com, or write to her at Brightstar Farm, POB 13501, Jackson, Wyoming 83002. If you have a story you would like to share, please enclose a stamped, self-addressed envelope.